Careers in Focus

Careers in Focus

PUBLISHING

THIRD EDITION

Ferguson

An imprint of Infobase Publishing

Careers in Focus: Publishing, Third Edition

Ferguson
An imprint of Infobase Publishing
132 West 31st Street
New York NY 10001

Library of Congress Cataloging-in-Publication Data

Careers in focus. Publishing—3rd ed.
    p. cm.
  Includes index.
  ISBN-13: 978-0-8160-6572-1 (acid-free paper)
  ISBN-10: 0-8160-6572-1 (acid-free paper) 1. Book industries and trade—Vocational guidance—United States—Juvenile literature. 2. Publishers and publishing—Vocational guidance—United States—Juvenile literature. I. J.G. Ferguson Publishing Company. II. Title: Publishing.
  Z471.C38 2007
  070.5'023'73—dc22   2007003665

Ferguson books are available at special discounts when purchased in bulk quantities for businesses, associations, institutions, or sales promotions. Please call our Special Sales Department in New York at (212) 967-8800 or (800) 322-8755.

You can find Ferguson on the World Wide Web at http://www.fergpubco.com

Text design by David Strelecky
Cover design by Salvatore Luongo

Printed in the United States of America

MP MSRF 10 9 8 7 6 5 4 3 2 1

This book is printed on acid-free paper.

Table of Contents

Introduction

The publishing industry can be broken down into categories, according to the kinds of publications that are produced by publishers: books, periodicals, and miscellaneous publications.

Generally speaking, a book consists of pages that have been bound in some way to form a single volume. The United Nations Educational, Scientific and Cultural Organization, which needed a definition in order to collect statistical data, decided that a book is "a nonperiodical printed publication of at least 49 pages excluding covers." Although there are many kinds of books, three of the largest categories of books are textbooks, trade books, and technical and professional books.

Periodicals are publications that appear at regular intervals, such as daily, weekly, monthly, and quarterly. The two major types of periodicals are newspapers and magazines. Although they are sometimes quite similar, newspapers tend to appear more frequently and to contain more time-sensitive information than magazines. In addition, newspapers are generally printed on relatively inexpensive paper and have large, unbound pages. Magazines, however, often use better and more expensive paper stock and are stapled or bound.

Other kinds of specialty publications include greeting cards, calendars, blank books, diaries, scheduling organizers, and postcards, to name only a few.

Internet publishing is increasing at an extremely rapid rate. Magazines, books, journals, and various other publications are being designed specifically for the Internet, and in many cases the entire texts of books are available to be downloaded. Some books and other publications are available only in electronic format. Internet publishing will no doubt continue to expand. Most traditional print publishers of any size also have a Web presence. Some publishers offer their publications online and use the Internet as a marketing tool, to promote and sell their publications.

In recent years, the publishing industry has also begun to produce nonprint-related products such as audio books, CD-ROMs, and other electronic media. This trend should continue during the next decade.

Publishing companies usually are divided into the following departments: editorial, which prepares written material and artwork for publication; production, which turns the material into the final printed piece; marketing, which promotes the product; sales, which sells the product; and the personnel, clerical, and accounting departments, which provide the organizational and financial support required by any business. Many newspapers and some other publishers have their own printing facilities, in which case they have a prepress department, which prepares the publication for printing, and a printing department. Most publishers, however, hire printers, bookbinders, and other specialists.

Employment in the publishing industry (excluding software) is expected to grow by 7 percent through 2014, or more slowly than the average for all industries, according to the U.S. Department of Labor (USDL). The USDL predicts slower-than-average growth in book, magazine, periodical, and miscellaneous publishing. Employment in textbook publishing will grow as a result of a growing number of high school and college students and the implementation of new teaching learning standards. Opportunities will also be good in technical and scientific publishing, as well as in custom publishing.

The Internet will play a significant role in the publishing industry in the next decade. More publishers are focusing on developing products for the Internet, as well as creating those in related media, such as e-books. As paper has become more expensive, publishers have become more motivated to provide products that do not require expenditures on paper. Similarly, newspaper and magazine publishers are seeking to increase their presence on the Web.

Each article in *Careers in Focus: Publishing* discusses a particular publishing-related career in detail. The articles appear in Ferguson's *Encyclopedia of Careers and Vocational Guidance,* but have been updated and revised with the latest information from the U.S. Department of Labor, professional organizations, and other sources. The following paragraphs detail the sections and features that appear in the book.

The **Quick Facts** section provides a brief summary of the career, including recommended school subjects, personal skills, work environment, minimum educational requirements, salary ranges, certification or licensing requirements, and employment outlook. This section also provides acronyms and identification numbers for the following government classification indexes: the Dictionary of Occupational Titles (DOT), the Guide to Occupational Exploration (GOE), the National Occupational Classification (NOC) Index, and the Occupational Information Network (O*NET)-Standard Occupational Classification System (SOC) index. The DOT, GOE, and O*NET-SOC indexes have been created by the U.S. government; the NOC index is Canada's career classification system. Readers can use the identification numbers listed in the Quick Facts section to access further information about a career. Print editions of the

DOT (*O*NET Dictionary of Occupational Titles.* Indianapolis, Ind.: JIST Works, 2004) and GOE (*The Complete Guide for Occupational Exploration.* Indianapolis, Ind.: JIST Works, 1993) are available at libraries. Electronic versions of the NOC (http://www23.hrdc-drhc.gc.ca) and O*NET-SOC (http://online.onetcenter.org) are available on the Internet. When no DOT, GOE, NOC, or O*NET-SOC numbers are present, this means that the U.S. Department of Labor or Human Resources Development Canada have not created a numerical designation for this career. In this instance, you will see the acronym "N/A," or not available.

The **Overview** section is a brief introductory description of the duties and responsibilities involved in this career. Oftentimes, a career may have a variety of job titles. When this is the case, alternative career titles are presented.

The **History** section describes the history of the particular job as it relates to the overall development of its industry or field.

The **Job** describes the primary and secondary duties of the job.

Requirements discusses high school and postsecondary education and training requirements, any certification or licensing that is necessary, and other personal requirements for success in the job.

Exploring offers suggestions on how to gain experience in or knowledge of the particular job before making a firm educational and financial commitment. The focus is on what can be done while still in high school (or in the early years of college) to gain a better understanding of the job.

The **Employers** section gives an overview of typical places of employment for the job.

Starting Out discusses the best ways to land that first job, be it through the college placement office, newspaper ads, or personal contact.

The **Advancement** section describes what kind of career path to expect from the job and how to get there.

Earnings lists salary ranges and describes the typical fringe benefits.

The **Work Environment** section describes the typical surroundings and conditions of employment—whether indoors or outdoors, noisy or quiet, social or independent. Also discussed are typical hours worked, any seasonal fluctuations, and the stresses and strains of the job.

The **Outlook** section summarizes the job in terms of the general economy and industry projections. For the most part, Outlook information is obtained from the U.S. Bureau of Labor Statistics and is supplemented by information taken from professional associations. Job growth terms follow those used in the *Occupational*

Outlook Handbook. Growth described as "much faster than the average" means an increase of 27 percent or more. Growth described as "faster than the average" means an increase of 18 to 26 percent. Growth described as "about as fast as the average" means an increase of 9 to 17 percent. Growth described as "more slowly than the average" means an increase of 0 to 8 percent. "Decline" means a decrease by any amount.

Each article ends with **For More Information,** which lists organizations that provide information on training, education, internships, scholarships, and job placement.

Careers in Focus: Publishing also includes photographs, informative sidebars, and interviews with professionals in the field.

Advertising Workers

QUICK FACTS

School Subjects
English
Psychology
Speech

Personal Skills
Artistic
Communication/ideas

Work Environment
Primarily indoors
Primarily one location

Minimum Education Level
Bachelor's degree

Salary Range
$21,080 to $43,060 to
$500,000+

Certification or Licensing
None available

Outlook
About as fast as the average

DOT
131

GOE
01.01.02

NOC
1122, 5121

O*NET-SOC
11-2011.00, 41-3011.00

OVERVIEW

Advertising is defined as mass communication paid for by an advertiser to persuade a particular segment of the public to adopt ideas or take actions of benefit to the advertiser. *Advertising workers* perform the various creative and business activities needed to take an advertisement from the research stage, to creative concept, through production, and finally to its intended audience. There are more than 154,000 advertising sales agents employed in the United States.

HISTORY

Advertising has been around as long as people have been exchanging goods and services. While a number of innovations spurred the development of advertising, it wasn't until the invention of the printing press in the 15th century that merchants began posting handbills in order to advertise their goods and services. By the 19th century, newspapers became an important means of advertising, followed by magazines in the late 1800s.

One of the problems confronting merchants in the early days of advertising was where to place their ads to generate the most business. In response, a number of people emerged who specialized in the area of advertising, accepting ads and posting them conspicuously. These agents were the first advertising workers. As competition among merchants increased, many of these agents offered to compose ads, as well as post them, for their clients.

Today, with intense competition among both new and existing businesses, advertising has become a necessity in the marketing of goods, property, and services alike. At the same time, the advertising worker's job has grown more demanding and complex than ever. With a wide variety of media from which advertisers can choose— including newspapers, magazines, billboards, radio, television, film and video, the World Wide Web, and a variety of other new technologies—today's advertising worker must not only develop and create ads and campaigns but keep abreast of current and developing buying and technology trends as well.

THE JOB

Approximately seven out of every 10 advertising organizations in the United States are full-service operations, offering their clients a broad range of services, including copywriting, graphics and other art-related work, production, media placement, and tracking and follow-up. These advertising agencies may have hundreds of people working in a dozen different departments, while smaller companies often employ just a handful of employees. Most agencies, however, have at least five departments: contact, research, media, creative, and production.

Contact department personnel are responsible for attracting new customers, and maintaining relationships with existing ones. Heading the contact department, *advertising agency managers* are concerned with the overall activities of the company. They formulate plans to generate business, by either soliciting new accounts or getting additional business from established clients. In addition, they meet with department heads to coordinate their operations and to create policies and procedures.

Advertising account executives are the contact department employees responsible for maintaining good relations between their clients and the agency. Acting as liaisons, they represent the agency to its clients and must therefore be able to communicate clearly and effectively. After examining the advertising objectives of their clients, account executives develop campaigns or strategies and then work with others from the various agency departments to target specific audiences, create advertising communications, and execute the campaigns. Presenting concepts, as well as the ad campaign at various stages of completion, to clients for their feedback and approval, account executives must have some knowledge of overall marketing strategies and be able to sell ideas.

Working with account executives, employees in the research department gather, analyze, and interpret the information needed to make a client's advertising campaign successful. By determining who the potential buyers of a product, property, or service will be, *research workers* predict which theme will have the most impact, what kind of packaging and price will have the most appeal, and which media will be the most effective.

Guided by a *research director,* research workers conduct local, regional, and national surveys in order to examine consumer preferences and then determine potential sales for the targeted product, property, or service based on those preferences. Researchers also gather information about competitors' prices, sales, and advertising methods.

Although research workers often recommend which media to use for an advertising campaign, *media planners* are the specialists who determine which print or broadcast media will be the most effective. Ultimately, they are responsible for choosing the combination of media that will reach the greatest number of potential buyers for the least amount of money, based on their clients' advertising strategies. Accordingly, planners must be familiar with the markets that each medium reaches, as well as the advantages and disadvantages of advertising in each.

Media buyers, often referred to as *space buyers* (for newspapers and magazines), or *time buyers* (for radio and television), do the actual purchasing of space and time according to a general plan formulated by the *media director.* In addition to ensuring that ads appear when and where they should, buyers negotiate costs for ad placement and maintain contact and extensive correspondence with clients and media representatives alike.

While the contact, research, and media departments handle the business side of a client's advertising campaign, the creative staff takes care of the artistic aspects. *Creative directors* oversee the activities of artists and writers and work with clients and account executives to determine the best advertising approaches, gain approval on concepts, and establish budgets and schedules.

Copywriters take the ideas submitted by creative directors and account executives and write descriptive text in the form of headlines, jingles, slogans, and other copy designed to attract the attention of potential buyers. In addition to being able to express themselves clearly and persuasively, copywriters must know what motivates people to buy. They must also be able to describe a product's features in a captivating and appealing way and be familiar with various advertising media. In large agencies, copywriters may be supervised by a copy chief.

Copywriters work closely with art directors to make sure that text and artwork create a unified, eye-catching arrangement. Planning the visual presentation of the client's message, from concept formulation to final artwork, the *art director* plays an important role in every stage of the creation of an advertising campaign. Art directors who work on filmed commercials and videos combine film techniques, music, and sound, as well as actors or animation, to communicate an advertiser's message. In publishing, art directors work with graphic designers, photographers, copywriters, and editors to develop brochures, catalogs, direct mail, and other printed pieces, all according to the advertising strategy.

Art directors must have a basic knowledge of graphics and design, computer software, printing, photography, and filmmaking. With the help of graphic artists, they decide where to place text and images, choose typefaces, and create storyboard ads and videos. Several layouts are usually submitted to the client, who chooses one or asks for revisions until a layout or conceptualization sketch meets with final approval. The art director then selects an illustrator, graphic artist, photographer, or TV or video producer, and the project moves on to the production department of the agency.

Production departments in large ad agencies may be divided into print production and broadcast production divisions, each with its own managers and staff. *Production managers* and their assistants convert and reproduce written copy and artwork into printed, filmed, or tape-recorded form so that they can be presented to the public. Production employees work closely with imaging, printing, engraving, and other art reproduction firms and must be familiar with various printing processes, papers, inks, typography, still and motion picture photography, digital imaging, and other processes and materials.

In addition to the principal employees in the five major departments, advertising organizations work with a variety of staff or freelance employees who have specialized knowledge, education, and skill, including photographers, photoengravers, typographers, printers, telemarketers, product and package designers, and producers of display materials. Finally, rounding out most advertising establishments are various support employees, such as production coordinators, video editors, word processors, statisticians, accountants, administrators, secretaries, and clerks.

The work of advertising employees is fast-paced, dynamic, and ever changing, depending on each client's strategies and budgets and the creative ideas generated by agency workers. In addition to innovative techniques, methods, media, and materials used by agency workers, new and emerging technologies are impacting the work of everyone in the advertising arena, from marketing executives to graphic designers. The Internet is undoubtedly the most revolutionary medium to hit the advertising scene. Through this worldwide, computer-based network, researchers are able to precisely target markets and clearly identify consumer needs. In addition, the Internet's Web pages provide media specialists with a powerful vehicle for advertising their clients' products, properties, and services. New technology has also been playing an important role in the creative area. Most art directors, for example, use a variety of computer software programs, and many create and oversee Web sites for their clients. Other interactive materials and vehicles, such as CD catalogs, touch-screens, and multidimensional visuals, are changing the way today's advertising workers are doing their jobs.

REQUIREMENTS

High School

You can prepare for a career as an advertising worker by taking a variety of courses at the high school level. General liberal arts courses, such as English, journalism, communications, economics, psychology, speech, business, social science, and mathematics, are important for aspiring advertising employees. In addition, those interested in the creative side of the field should take such classes as art, drawing, graphic design, illustration, and art history. Finally, since computers play a vital role in the advertising field, you should become familiar with word processing and layout programs, as well as the World Wide Web.

Postsecondary Training

The American Association of Advertising Agencies notes that most agencies employing entry-level personnel prefer college graduates. Copywriters are best prepared with a college degree in English, journalism, or communications; research workers need college training in statistics, market research, and social studies; and most account executives have business or related degrees. Media positions are increasingly requiring a college degree in communications or a technology-related area. Media directors and research directors with a master's degree have a distinct advantage over those with only an undergraduate degree. Some research department heads even have doctorates.

While the requirements from agency to agency may vary somewhat, graduates of liberal arts colleges or those with majors in fields such as communications, journalism, business administration, or marketing research are preferred. Good language skills, as well as a broad liberal arts background, are necessary for advertising workers. College students interested in the field should therefore take such courses as English, writing, art, philosophy, foreign languages, social studies, sociology, psychology, economics, mathematics, statistics, advertising, and marketing. Some 900 degree-granting institutions throughout the United States offer specialized majors in advertising as part of their curriculum.

Other Requirements

In addition to the variety of educational and work experiences necessary for those aspiring to advertising careers, many personal characteristics are also important. Although you will perform many tasks of your job independently as an advertising worker, you will also interact with others as part of a team. In addition to working with other staff members, you may be responsible for initiating and maintaining client contact. You must therefore be able to get along well with people and communicate clearly.

Advertising is not a job that involves routine, and you must be able to meet and adjust to the challenges presented by each new client. The ability to think clearly and logically is important, because commonsense approaches rather than gimmicks persuade people that something is worth buying. You must also be creative, flexible, and imaginative in order to anticipate consumer demand and trends, to develop effective concepts, and to sell the properties or services of your clients.

Finally, with technology evolving at breakneck speed, it's vital that you keep pace with technological advances and trends. In addition to being able to work with the most current software and hardware, you should be familiar with the Web, as well as with other technology that is impacting—and will continue to impact—the industry.

EXPLORING

If you aspire to a career in the advertising industry, you can gain valuable insight by taking writing and art courses offered either in school or by private organizations. In addition to the theoretical ideas and techniques that such classes provide, you can actually apply what you learn by working full or part time at local department stores or newspaper offices. Some advertising agencies or research firms also employ students to interview people or to conduct other market research. Work as an agency clerk or messenger may also be available. Participating in internships at an advertising or marketing organization is yet another way to explore the field, as well as to determine your aptitude for advertising work. You may find it helpful to read publications dedicated to this industry, such as *Advertising Age* (http://www.adage.com).

EMPLOYERS

More than 154,000 advertising sales workers are employed in the United States. Most advertising workers are employed by advertising agencies that plan and prepare advertising material for their clients on a commission or service fee basis. However, some large companies and nearly all department stores prefer to handle their own advertising. Advertising workers in such organizations prepare advertising materials for in-house clients, such as the marketing or catalog department. They also may be involved in the planning, preparation, and production of special promotional materials, such as sales brochures, articles describing the activities of the organization, or Web sites. Some advertising workers are employed by owners of various media, including newspapers, magazines, radio and television networks, and outdoor advertising. Workers employed in these media are mainly sales representatives who sell advertising space or broadcast time to advertising agencies or companies that maintain their own advertising departments.

In addition to agencies, large companies, and department stores, advertising services and supply houses employ such advertising specialists as photographers, photoengravers, typographers, printers, product and package designers, display producers, and others who assist in the production of various advertising materials.

According to the American Association of Advertising Agencies, there are more than 13,000 advertising agencies in the United States. Most of the large firms are located in Chicago, Los Angeles, and New York. Employment opportunities are also available, however, at a variety of "small shops," four out of five of which employ fewer than 10 workers each. In addition, a growing number of self-employment and home-based business opportunities are resulting in a variety of industry jobs located in outlying areas rather than in big cities.

STARTING OUT

Although competition for advertising jobs is fierce and getting your foot in the door can be difficult, there are a variety of ways to launch a career in the field. Some large advertising agencies recruit college graduates and place them in training programs designed to acquaint beginners with all aspects of advertising work, but these opportunities are limited and highly competitive.

Instead, many graduates simply send resumes to businesses that employ entry-level advertising workers. Newspapers, radio and television stations, printers, photographers, and advertising agencies are but a few of the businesses that will hire beginners. The *Standard Directory of Advertising Agencies* (New Providence, N.J.: National Register Publishing Company, 2003) lists the names and addresses of ad agencies all across the nation. You can find the directory in almost any public library.

Those who have had work experience in sales positions often enter the advertising field as account executives. High school graduates and other people without experience who want to work in advertising, however, may find it necessary to begin as clerks or assistants to research and production staff members or to copywriters.

ADVANCEMENT

The career path in an advertising agency generally leads from trainee to skilled worker to division head and then to department head. It may also take employees from department to department, allowing them to gain more responsibility with each move. Opportunities abound for those with talent, leadership capability, and ambition.

Management positions require experience in all aspects of advertising, including agency work, communication with advertisers, and knowledge of various advertising media. Copywriters, account executives, and other advertising agency workers who demonstrate outstanding ability to deal with clients and supervise coworkers usually have a good chance of advancing to management positions. Other workers, however, prefer to acquire specialized skills. For them, advancement may mean more responsibility, the opportunity to perform more specialized tasks, and increased pay.

Advertising workers at firms that have their own advertising departments can also earn promotions. Advancement in any phase of advertising work is usually dependent on the employee's experience, training, and demonstrated skills.

Some qualified copywriters, artists, and account executives establish their own agencies or become marketing consultants. For these entrepreneurs, advancement may take the form of an increasing number of accounts and/or more prestigious clients.

EARNINGS

Salaries of advertising workers vary depending on the type of work, the size of the agency, its geographic location, the kind of accounts handled, and the agency's gross earnings. Salaries are also determined by a worker's education, aptitude, and experience. The wide range of jobs in advertising makes it difficult to estimate average salaries for all positions.

According to a survey by the National Association of Colleges and Employers, marketing majors entering the job market in 2005 had average starting salaries of $33,873, while advertising majors averaged $31,340.

The U.S. Department of Labor reports that the mean annual earnings for advertising sales agents who were employed at newspaper, directory, and book publishers has mean annual earnings of $43,910 in 2005. The lowest paid 10 percent of all advertising sales agents earned less than $21,080, while the highest paid advertising sales agents earned more than $89,710. In advertising agencies, an executive vice president can earn from $113,000 to $500,000 a year or more. Account executives earned a median of $57,000, while senior account executives earned a median of $73,000. In the research and media departments, media directors earn a median of $102,000, and media planners and buyers between $40,000 and $45,000 per year. In the creative department, art directors earn a median of $73,000 or more annually. Salaries for relatively glamorous jobs at agencies can be low, due to high competition. In advertising departments at other businesses and industries, individual earnings vary widely. Salaries of advertising workers are generally higher, however, at consumer product firms than at industrial product organizations because of the competition among consumer product producers. The majority of companies offer insurance benefits, a retirement plan, and other incentives and bonuses.

WORK ENVIRONMENT

Conditions at most agencies are similar to those found in other offices throughout the country, except that employees must frequently work under great pressure to meet deadlines. While a traditional 40-hour workweek is the norm at some companies, almost half (44 percent) of advertising, marketing, promotions, public relations, and sales managers report that they work more hours per week, including evenings and weekends. Bonuses and time off during slow periods are sometimes provided as a means of compensation for unusual workloads and hours.

Although some advertising employees, such as researchers, work independently on a great many tasks, most must function as part of a team. With frequent meetings with coworkers, clients, and media representatives alike, the work environment is usually energized, with ideas being exchanged, contracts being negotiated, and schedules being modified.

Did You Know?

The Association of American Publishers estimated that U.S. book sales were more than $25 billion in 2005—an increase of 9.9 percent over 2004 sales. Overall, trade sales increased 24.9 percent, with sales of juvenile books showing the largest growth. Sales of e-books increased by nearly 45 percent. Industry segments that showed declines included book clubs/mail order (-6.7 percent), religious (-6.1 percent), and professional (-1.0 percent).

Advertising work is fast-paced and exciting. As a result, many employees often feel stressed out as they are constantly challenged to take initiative and be creative. Nevertheless, advertising workers enjoy both professional and personal satisfaction in seeing the culmination of their work communicated to sometimes millions of people.

OUTLOOK

Employment for advertising sales workers is expected to grow about as fast as the average for all occupations through 2014, according to the U.S. Department of Labor. Network and cable television, radio, newspapers, the Web, and certain other media (particularly interactive vehicles) will offer advertising workers an increasing number of employment opportunities. Some media, such as magazines, direct mail, and event marketing, are expected to provide fewer job opportunities.

Advertising agencies will enjoy faster than average employment growth, as will industries that service ad agencies and other businesses in the advertising field, such as those that offer commercial photography, imaging, art, and graphics services.

At the two extremes, enormous "mega-agencies" and small shops employing up to only 10 workers each offer employment opportunities for people with experience, talent, flexibility, and drive. In addition, self-employment and home-based businesses are on the rise. In general, openings will become available to replace workers who change positions, retire, or leave the field for other reasons. Competition for these jobs will be keen, however, because of the large number of qualified professionals in this traditionally desirable field. Opportunities will be best for the well-qualified and well-trained applicant. Employers favor college graduates with experience, a high level of creativity, and strong communications skills. People who are not well qualified or prepared for agency work will find the advertising field increasingly difficult to enter. The same is also true for those who seek work in companies that service ad agencies.

FOR MORE INFORMATION

For information on student chapters, scholarships, and internships, contact
American Advertising Federation
1101 Vermont Avenue, NW, Suite 500
Washington, DC 20005-6306
Tel: 202-898-0089
Email: aaf@aaf.org
http://www.aaf.org

For industry information, contact
American Association of Advertising Agencies
405 Lexington, 18th Floor
New York, NY 10174-1801
Tel: 212-682-2500
http://www.aaaa.org

For career and salary information, contact
American Marketing Association
311 South Wacker Drive, Suite 5800
Chicago, IL 60606-6629
Tel: 800-262-1150
Email: info@ama.org
http://www.marketingpower.com

The Art Directors Club is an international, nonprofit organization for creatives in advertising, graphic design, interactive media, broadcast design, typography, packaging, environmental design, photography, illustration, and related disciplines.
The Art Directors Club
106 West 29th Street
New York, NY 10001-5301
Tel: 212-643-1440
Email: info@adcglobal.org
http://www.adcglobal.org

For information on student membership and careers, contact
Direct Marketing Educational Foundation
1120 Avenue of the Americas

New York, NY 10036-6700
Tel: 212-768-7277
http://www.the-dma.org/dmef

The Graphic Artists Guild promotes and protects the economic interests of the artist/designer and is committed to improving conditions for all creators of graphic art and raising standards for the entire industry.
Graphic Artists Guild
32 Broadway, Suite 1114
New York, NY 10004-1612
Tel: 212-791-3400
http://www.gag.org

Art Directors

OVERVIEW

Art directors play a key role in every stage of the creation of an advertisement or ad campaign, from formulating concepts to supervising production. Ultimately, they are responsible for planning and overseeing the presentation of their clients' messages in print or on screen—that is, in books, magazines, newspapers, television commercials, posters, and packaging, as well as in film and video and on the Internet.

In publishing, art directors work with artists, photographers, and text editors to develop visual images and generate copy, according to the marketing strategy. They are responsible for evaluating existing illustrations, determining presentation styles and techniques, hiring both staff and freelance talent, working with layouts, and preparing budgets.

In sum, art directors are charged with selling to, informing, and educating consumers. They supervise both in-house and off-site staff, handle executive issues, and oversee the entire artistic production process. There are approximately 71,000 art directors working in the United States.

HISTORY

Artists have always been an important part of the creative process throughout history. Medieval monks illuminated their manuscripts, painting with egg-white tempera on vellum. Each copy of each book had to be printed and illustrated individually.

Printed illustrations first appeared in books in 1461. Through the years, prints were made through woodblock, copperplate, lithography, and other means of duplicating images. Although making many copies of the same illustration was now possible, publishers still depended on individual artists to create the original works. Text editors usually decided what was to be illustrated and how, while artists commonly supervised the production of the artwork.

The first art directors were probably staff illustrators for book publishers. As the publishing industry grew more complex and incorporated new technologies such as photography and film, art direction evolved into a more supervisory position and became a full-time job. Publishers and advertisers began to need specialists who could acquire and use illustrations and photos. Women's magazines, such as *Vogue* and *Harper's Bazaar,* and photo magazines, such as *National Geographic,* relied so much on illustration and photography that the photo editor and art director began to carry as much power as the text editor.

Today's art directors supervise almost every type of visual project produced. Through a variety of methods and media, from magazines and comic books to newspapers and the Internet, art directors communicate ideas by selecting and supervising every element that goes into the finished product.

THE JOB

Art directors are responsible for all visual aspects of on-screen or printed projects. The art director oversees the process of developing visual solutions to a variety of communication problems. He or she helps to advertise products and services; enhance books, magazines, newsletters, and other publications; and create television commercials, film and video productions, and Web sites. Some art directors with experience or knowledge in specific fields specialize in such areas as packaging, exhibitions and displays, or the Internet. But all directors, even those with specialized backgrounds, must be skilled in and knowledgeable about design, illustration, photography, computers, research, and writing in order to supervise the work of graphic artists, photographers, copywriters, text editors, and other employees.

In print advertising and publishing, art directors may begin with the client's concept or develop one in collaboration with the copywriter and account executive. Once the concept is established, the next step is to decide on the most effective way to communicate it. If there is text, for example, should the art director choose illustrations based on specific text references, or should the illustrations fill in the gaps in the copy? If a piece is being revised, existing illustrations must be reevaluated.

After deciding what needs to be illustrated, art directors must find sources that can create or provide the art. Photo agencies, for example, have photographs and illustrations on thousands of different subjects. If, however, the desired illustration does not exist, it may have to be commissioned or designed by one of the staff designers. Commissioning artwork means that the art director contacts a photographer or illustrator and explains what is needed. A price is negotiated, and the artist creates the image specifically for the art director.

Once the illustrations and other art elements have been secured, they must be presented in an appealing manner. The art director supervises (and may help in the production of) the layout of the piece and presents the final version to the client or creative director. Laying out is the process of figuring out where every image, headline, and block of text will be placed on the page. The size, style, and method of reproduction must all be specifically indicated so that the image is recreated as the director intended it.

Technology is playing an increasingly important role in the art director's job. Most art directors, for example, use a variety of computer software programs, including Adobe InDesign, PageMaker, FrameMaker, Illustrator, and Photoshop; QuarkXPress; and Corel-DRAW. Many others create and oversee Web sites for clients and work with other interactive media and materials, including CD-ROM, touch-screens, multidimensional visuals, and new animation programs.

Art directors usually work on more than one project at a time and must be able to keep numerous, unrelated details straight. They often work under pressure of a deadline and yet must remain calm and pleasant when dealing with clients and staff. Because they are supervisors, art directors are often called upon to resolve problems, not only with projects but with employees as well.

Art directors are not entry-level workers. They usually have years of experience working at lower-level jobs in the field before gaining the knowledge needed to supervise projects. Depending on whether they work primarily in film, television, or publishing, art directors have to know how film is processed or digitally mastered or how printing presses operate. They should also be familiar with a variety of production techniques in order to understand the wide range of ways that images can be manipulated to meet the needs of a project.

REQUIREMENTS

High School

A college degree is usually a requirement for art directors; however, in some instances, it is not absolutely necessary. A variety of high school courses will give you both a taste of college-level offerings and an idea of the skills necessary for art directors on the job. These courses include art, drawing, art history, graphic design, illustration, photography, advertising, and desktop publishing.

Other useful courses that you should take in high school include business, computing, drama, English, technical drawing, cultural studies, psychology, and social science.

Postsecondary Training

Courses in photography, filmmaking, set direction, advertising, marketing, layout, desktop publishing, and fashion are also important for those interested in becoming art directors. Specialized courses, sometimes offered only at professional film or art schools, may be particularly helpful for students who want to go into art direction. These include animation, storyboard, typography, Web site design, and portfolio development.

Because of the rapidly increasing use of computers in design work, it is essential to have a thorough understanding of how computer art and layout programs work. In smaller companies, the art director may be responsible for operating this equipment; in larger companies, a staff person, under the direction of the art director, may use these programs. In either case, the director must know what can be done with the available equipment.

In addition to course work at the college level, many universities and professional art schools offer graduates or students in their final year a variety of workshop projects, desktop publishing training opportunities, and internships. These programs provide students with opportunities to develop their personal design styles as well as their portfolios.

Other Requirements

The work of an art director requires creativity, imagination, curiosity, and a sense of adventure. Art directors must be able to work with all sorts of specialized equipment and computer software, such as graphic design programs, as well as make presentations on the ideas behind their work.

The ability to work well with different people and organizations is a must for art directors. They must always be up to date on new techniques, trends, and attitudes. And because deadlines are a constant part of the work, an ability to handle stress and pressure well is key.

Other requirements for art directors include time management skills and an interest in media and people's motivations and lifestyles.

EXPLORING

High school students can get an idea of what an art director does by working on the staff of the school newspaper, magazine, or yearbook, and developing their own Web sites or zines. It may also be possible to secure a part-time job assisting the advertising director of your local newspaper or to work at an advertising agency. Developing your own artistic talent is important, and this can be accomplished through self-training (reading books and practicing); through courses in painting, drawing, or other creative arts; or by working with a group of friends to create a publication. At the very least, you should develop your "creative eye," that is, your ability to develop ideas visually. One way to do this is by familiarizing yourself with great works, such as paintings or highly creative magazines, books, motion pictures, videos, or commercials.

EMPLOYERS

Approximately 71,000 art directors are employed in the United States. A variety of organizations in virtually all industries employ art directors. They might work at advertising agencies, publishing houses, museums, packaging firms, photography studios, marketing and public relations firms, desktop publishing outfits, digital pre-press houses, or printing companies. Art directors who oversee and produce on-screen products often work for film production houses, Web designers, multimedia developers, computer games developers, or television stations.

STARTING OUT

Since an art director's job requires a great deal of experience, it is usually not considered an entry-level position. Typically, a person on a career track toward art director is hired as an assistant to an established director. Recent graduates wishing to enter the field should have a portfolio containing samples of their work to demonstrate their understanding of both the business and the media in which they want to work.

Serving as an intern is a good way to get experience and develop skills. Graduates should also consider taking an entry-level job in a publisher's art department to gain initial experience. Either way, aspiring art directors must be willing to acquire their credentials by working on various projects. This may mean working in a variety of areas, such as advertising, marketing, editing, and design.

ADVANCEMENT

While some may be content upon reaching the position of art director to remain there, many art directors take on even more responsibility within their organizations, start their own advertising agencies, create their own Web sites, develop original multimedia programs, or launch their own magazines.

Many people who get to the position of art director do not advance beyond the title but move on to work on more prestigious films or at better-known firms. Competition for top positions continues to be keen because of the sheer number of talented people interested. At smaller publications or local companies, the competition may be less intense, since candidates are competing primarily against others in the local market.

EARNINGS

According to the U.S. Department of Labor, beginning art directors or an art director who worked at a small firm earned $36,610 or less per year in 2005; experienced art directors working at larger companies earned more than $125,890. Mean annual earnings for art directors employed in newspaper, book, and directory publishing were $63,950 in 2005. Most companies employing art directors offer insurance benefits, a retirement plan, and other incentives and bonuses. Freelance art directors are usually responsible for providing their own health insurance and other benefits.

WORK ENVIRONMENT

Art directors usually work in studios or office buildings. While their work areas are ordinarily comfortable, well lit, and ventilated, they often handle glue, paint, ink, and other materials that pose safety hazards, and they should, therefore, exercise caution.

Art directors at art and design studios and publishing firms usually work a standard 40-hour week. Many, however, work overtime during busy periods in order to meet deadlines. Similarly, directors at film and video operations and at television studios work as many hours as required—usually many more than 40 per week—in order to finish projects according to predetermined schedules.

While art directors work independently while reviewing artwork and reading copy, much of their time is spent collaborating with and supervising a team of employees, often consisting of copywriters, editors, photographers, graphic artists, and account executives.

OUTLOOK

The extent to which art director positions are in demand, like many other positions, depends on the economy in general; when times are tough, people and businesses spend less, and cutbacks are made. When the economy is healthy, employment prospects for art directors will be favorable. The U.S. Department of Labor predicts that employment for art directors will grow about as fast as the average for all other occupations through 2014. One area that shows particularly good promise for growth is the retail industry, since more and more large retail establishments, especially catalog houses, will be employing in-house advertising art directors. And people working with new media are increasingly looking for artists and directors to promote new and existing products and services, enhance their Web sites, develop new multimedia programs, and create multidimensional visuals. People who can quickly and creatively generate new concepts and ideas will be in high demand.

However, it is important to note that the supply of aspiring artists is expected to exceed the number of job openings. As a result, those wishing to enter the field will encounter keen competition for salaried, staff positions as well as for freelance work. And although the Internet is expected to provide many opportunities for artists and art directors, some firms are hiring employees without formal art or design training to operate computer-aided design systems and oversee work.

FOR MORE INFORMATION

For more information on design professionals, contact
American Institute of Graphic Arts
164 Fifth Avenue
New York, NY 10010-5901
Tel: 212-807-1990
http://www.aiga.org

The Art Directors Club is an international, nonprofit organization of directors in advertising, graphic design, interactive media, broadcast design, typography, packaging, environmental design, photography, illustration, and related disciplines. For information, contact
The Art Directors Club
106 West 29th Street
New York, NY 10001-5301
Tel: 212-643-1440

Email: info@adcglobal.org
http://www.adcglobal.org

For information on the graphic arts, contact
Graphic Artists Guild
32 Broadway, Suite 1114
New York, NY 10004-1612
Tel: 212-791-3400
http://www.gag.org

Bindery Workers

OVERVIEW

Binding, or finishing, is the final step in the printing process. *Bindery workers* take the printed pages that go into books, magazines, pamphlets, catalogs, and other materials and fold, cut, sew, staple, stitch, and/or glue them together to produce the finished product.

Bindery workers typically work in commercial printing plants or specialized bindery shops. Some bindery workers perform highly specialized tasks that require a certain amount of training; other bindery workers perform simple, repetitive tasks that are easily mastered. Approximately 81,000 people are employed in bindery work in the United States.

HISTORY

Bookbinding is an ancient and honored craft. As early as the third century A.D., when books were still written on papyrus and animal skins, pages of parchment manuscripts were stored between two boards. During the Middle Ages, bookbinding was developed into a fine art by monks in monasteries who decorated the board covers of sacred books with elaborate bindings made of metal, jewels, ivory, and enamel.

Around the year 900, the English introduced the use of leather to cover the boards and soon became leaders in this field. English kings employed binders to decorate the books in the royal library. Nobles and other powerful figures followed their monarchs' lead and established their own libraries of luxuriously bound volumes. These fine bindings were usually decorated with coats of arms or family crests. In this way, the bookbinder became a highly regarded artist.

A worker makes an adjustment on a Harris Stitcher-Timmer bindery machine. *(Jim West Photography)*

With the invention of the printing press in the 15th century, the demand for books grew among ordinary citizens, and the making and binding of books was transferred from monasteries and palaces to the shops of printers and binders.

Today, the art of hand bookbinding is increasingly rare. There are still shops where skilled workers bind rare and restored books, but most finishing is now highly automated both for books and for other printed pieces.

THE JOB

The average bindery worker today is a skilled machine operator. Collating, inserting, and other bindery tasks are periodically done by hand, but the bulk of binding processes are automated: cutting, folding, gathering, stitching, gluing, trimming, and wrapping. Finishing also might include embossing, die cutting, and foil stamping.

There are several different types of binderies: *edition binderies,* which specialize in large volumes of books and magazines; *pamphlet binderies,* which make pamphlets; *trade* or *job binderies,* which finish smaller quantities on a contract basis for printers and publishers; and *manifold* or *loose-leaf binderies,* which bind blank pages and forms into ledgers, notebooks, checkbooks, calendars, and notepads. *Hand bookbinders* work in small shops where they bind special-edition books or restore and rebind old books. Hand bookbinding offers a wide variety of projects.

Bindery work ranges from simple to complex. Some binding jobs, such as preparing leaflets or newspaper inserts, require only a single step—in this case folding. The most complicated binding work is edition binding, or the production of books from large printed sheets of paper. Book pages are usually not produced individually but are printed on a large sheet of paper, six or eight at a time. These large sheets are folded by a machine into units called signatures, and the signatures are joined together in the proper order to make a complete book. The signatures are then assembled by a gathering machine and sewed or glued together to make what is called a book block. The book blocks are compressed in a machine to ensure compactness and uniform thickness, trimmed to the proper size, and reinforced with fabric strips that are glued along the spine. The covers for the book are created separately and are pasted or glued to the book block by machine. Books may undergo a variety of finishing operations, such as gilding the edges of pages or wrapping with dust jackets, before they are inspected and packed for shipment. A similar procedure is used in the binding of magazines, catalogs, and directories.

In large binderies, the operations are usually done in an assembly-line fashion by workers who are trained in just one or two procedures. For example, a *stitcher operator* runs the machines that stitch printed matter along its spine or edge. Other workers might specialize in the cutting, folding, or gathering processes. Much of this work involves setting up equipment and adjusting it as needed during the binding process.

REQUIREMENTS

High School
People with some knowledge of printing and binding are likely to have an advantage when they apply for jobs in the field. High school students interested in bindery careers can gain some exposure to bindery work by taking shop courses or attending a vocational-technical high school.

Postsecondary Training
Occupational skill centers, often operated by unions, can also provide an introduction to the industry. Postsecondary training in graphic arts, often offered at community and junior colleges, is also useful. Local offices of printing industry associations offer individual courses related to the field.

Formal apprenticeships are becoming less common but are available for workers interested in acquiring highly specialized skills. A four-year apprenticeship is usually needed to learn how to restore and bind rare books.

Shorter apprenticeship programs combining on-the-job training with classroom instruction may be required for union shops. Four-year college programs in graphic arts are recommended for people who want to work in bindery shop management. With today's fast-changing technology, all bindery workers are likely to need occasional retraining once employed in a job.

Certification or Licensing

The National Council for Skill Standards in Graphic Communications has established a voluntary certification program for expert-level, high-tech bindery operators who have at least three years of full-time saddle stitching experience. Applicants who successfully pass an examination receive the national council certified operator designation.

Other Requirements

Accuracy, neatness, patience, and good eyesight are among the qualities needed for bindery occupations. Careful attention to detail may be the most important requirement for a bindery worker. Errors made in this final stage of the printing process can be costly if it means reinvesting labor and materials to redo previous steps. Finger dexterity is essential for workers who count, insert, paste, and fold, while mechanical skill is required of those who operate automated equipment. Artistic ability and imagination are required for hand bookbinding. In general, employers look for individuals with good communication skills and strong mathematical and mechanical aptitude.

EXPLORING

You may be able to find out firsthand about bindery work through a summer job in a local bindery. By observing operations and talking with experienced employees, you can both learn and earn.

In addition, many trade and vocational schools offer courses that teach the basics of the trade. Some schools even have work-study arrangements with trade or job binderies that enable students to broaden their experience in the field. Contacts made during this training period may be useful in securing full-time employment after graduation.

Industry experts say that any exposure to the printing industry is valuable background for a job in the bindery field.

EMPLOYERS

Of the approximately 81,000 bindery workers in the United States, the majority are employed in commercial printing plants. In addition, a large number of bindery workers are employed at bindery trade shops. These shops provide binding services for printers without binderies or printers with too much binding work to complete on their own. Bindery work is done in printing plants, which may be located in out-of-the-way places where materials and labor are cheaper.

STARTING OUT

Information on apprenticeships and training opportunities is available through the state employment service, binderies, or local chapters of printing industry associations.

People who want to start working first and learn their skills on the job should contact potential employers directly, especially if they want to work in a small nonunion bindery. Openings for trainee positions may be listed in newspaper want ads or with the state employment service. Trade school graduates may find jobs through their school's career services office. And industry association offices often run job listing services.

ADVANCEMENT

Most bindery workers learn their craft through on-the-job training. Entry-level employees start by doing simple tasks, such as moving paper from cutting machines to folding machines. As workers gain experience, they advance to more difficult tasks and learn how to handle one or more finishing processes. It generally takes one to three months to learn how to operate a new piece of equipment.

Skilled workers can advance to supervisory positions, but opportunities for this type of advancement are mostly limited to larger binderies. Advancement is likely to be faster for workers who have completed an apprenticeship program than for those who have learned skills solely through on-the-job training.

EARNINGS

Bindery workers' earnings vary according to the type of work they do, where they live, and if they are covered by union contracts.

The U.S. Department of Labor reports that bindery workers had median hourly wages of $12.04 in 2005. This wage translates in approximately $25,050 per year for full-time work. The lowest paid 10 percent earned less than $7.78 per hour (approximately $16,190 annually) that same year. At the top of the pay scale, the highest paid 10 percent made more than $19.94 per hour (approximately $41,470 per year).

Skilled bookbinders who finish books by hand tend to earn more money: a median salary of $14.04 per hour, or $29,200 per year. The lowest 10 percent of bookbinders made $8.21 per hour, or $17,080 per year, while the highly skilled bookbinders in the upper 10 percent made $21.21 per hour, or $44,120 per year.

Workers under union contracts usually have higher earnings. The average workweek for bindery workers is between 35 and 40 hours, although many work more than that. Generally, full-time employees are paid overtime wages if they work more than 40 hours. Benefits typically include health insurance, paid vacation time, and retirement plans.

WORK ENVIRONMENT

Modern binderies are usually well lighted and well ventilated, but they are often noisy. Certain jobs can be strenuous, requiring workers to stand for long periods of time and repeatedly reach, stoop, kneel, and lift and carry heavy items. Because many tasks are done in an assembly-line manner, bindery workers must be able to tolerate doing repetitious, monotonous tasks.

OUTLOOK

The U.S. Department of Labor predicts employment for bindery workers will decline through 2014. Because the binding process is becoming increasingly mechanized, the need for workers to do certain tasks is dwindling. New, automated equipment in binderies can perform a number of operations in sequence, beginning with raw stock at one end of the process and finishing with the final product. These machines shorten production time, increase plant productivity, and reduce overall labor requirements. Furthermore, the entire publishing industry is cutting back on expenses, looking to shave costs however possible. This tends to create a tight market environment for its manufacturing end.

Knowledgeable workers, however, are needed to oversee the use of new technologies. Those with up-to-date computer skills and mechanical aptitude will have the best opportunities in the field.

"The pace of the industry has changed dramatically," says Bob Goodman of Zonne Bookbinders in Chicago, Illinois. "It used to be that a job was scheduled over three or four weeks. Now everything is needed 'by tomorrow.'" Because of this faster pace, Goodman says many binderies rely heavily on temporary workers to complete large jobs quickly.

Most full-time job opportunities will come from the need to replace workers who leave the field for different jobs, retirement, or other reasons.

FOR MORE INFORMATION

This trade association represents trade binders, loose-leaf manufacturers, and suppliers throughout the United States, Canada, and Europe. For industry news and other resources, contact:
Binding Industries Association International
200 Deer Run Road
Sewickley, PA 15143-2324
http://www.bindingindustries.org

This union represents U.S. and Canadian workers in all craft and skill areas of the printing and publishing industries. For information on education and training programs available through local union schools, contact
Graphic Communications Conference of the International
Brotherhood of Teamsters
1900 L Street, NW
Washington, DC 20036-5002
Tel: 202-462-1400
http://www.gciu.org

For information on certification, contact
National Council for Skill Standards in Graphic Communications
Harry V. Quadracci Printing & Graphic Center
800 Main Street
Pewaukee, WI 53072-4601
Tel: 262-695-3470
http://www.ncssgc.org

This coalition serves as a clearinghouse, resource center, and coordinator of programs promoting career awareness, training, and a positive industry image.
NPES – The Association for Suppliers of Printing, Publishing, and Converting Technologies

1899 Preston White Drive
Reston, VA 20191-5468
Tel: 703-264-7200
Email: npes@npes.org
http://www.npes.org

*For information on education and careers in the graphic communi-
cations industry, visit*
Graphic COMM Central
http://teched.vt.edu/gcc

Columnists

OVERVIEW

Columnists write opinion pieces for publication in newspapers or magazines. Some columnists work for syndicates, which are organizations that sell articles to many media at once.

Columnists can be generalists who write about whatever strikes them on any topic. Most columnists focus on a specialty, such as government, politics, local issues, health, humor, sports, gossip, or other themes.

Most newspapers employ local columnists or run columns from syndicates. Some syndicated columnists work out of their homes or private offices.

HISTORY

Because the earliest American newspapers were political vehicles, much of their news stories brimmed with commentary and opinion. This practice continued up until the Civil War. Horace Greeley, a popular editor who had regularly espoused partisanship in his *New York Tribune*, was the first to give editorial opinion its own page separate from the news.

As newspapers grew into instruments of mass communication, their editors sought balance and fairness on the editorial pages and began publishing a number of columns with varying viewpoints.

Famous Washington, D.C.-based columnist Jack Anderson was known for bringing an investigative slant to the editorial page. Art Buchwald and Molly Ivins became well known for their satirical look at government and politicians.

The growth of news and commentary on the Internet has only added to the power of columnists.

QUICK FACTS

School Subjects
Computer science
English
Journalism

Personal Skills
Communication/ideas
Helping/teaching

Work Environment
Indoors and outdoors
Primarily multiple locations

Minimum Education Level
Bachelor's degree

Salary Range
$18,300 to $32,270 to $71,220+

Certification or Licensing
None available

Outlook
More slowly than the average

DOT
131

GOE
01.01.03

NOC
5123

O*NET-SOC
27-3022.00, 27-3043.00

Richard Roeper speaks during a ceremony honoring film critic Roger Ebert. *(Michael Germana/Landov)*

THE JOB

Columnists often take news stories and enhance the facts with personal opinions and panache. Columnists may also write from their personal experiences. Either way, a column usually has a punchy start, a pithy middle, and a strong, sometimes poignant, ending.

Columnists are responsible for writing columns on a regular basis on accord with a schedule, depending on the frequency of publication. They may write a column daily, weekly, quarterly, or monthly. Like other journalists, they face pressure to meet a deadline.

Most columnists are free to select their own story ideas. The need to constantly come up with new and interesting ideas may be one of the hardest parts of the job, but also one of the most rewarding. Columnists search through newspapers, magazines, and the Internet, watch television, and listen to the radio. The various types of media suggest ideas and keep the writer aware of current events and social issues.

Next, they do research, delving into a topic much like an investigative reporter would, so that they can back up their arguments with facts.

Finally, they write, usually on a computer. After a column is written, at least one editor goes over it to check for clarity and correct mistakes. Then the cycle begins again. Often a columnist will write a few relatively timeless pieces to keep for use as backups in a pinch, in case a new idea can't be found or falls through.

Most columnists work in newsrooms or magazine offices, although some, especially those who are syndicated but not affiliated with a particular newspaper, work out of their homes or private offices. Many well-known syndicated columnists work out of Washington, D.C.

Newspapers often run small pictures of columnists, called head shots, next to their columns. This, and a consistent placement of a column in a particular spot in the paper, usually gives a columnist greater recognition than a reporter or editor.

REQUIREMENTS

High School

You'll need a broad-based education to do this job well, so take a college prep curriculum in high school. Concentrate on English and journalism classes that will help you develop research and writing skills. Keep your computer skills up to date with computer science courses. History, psychology, science, and math should round out your education. Are you interested in a particular topic, such as sports, politics, or developments in medicine? Then take classes that will help you develop your knowledge in that area. In the future, you'll be able to draw on this knowledge when you write your column.

Postsecondary Training

As is the case for other journalists, at least a bachelor's degree in journalism is usually required, although some journalists have earned degrees in political science or English. Experience may be gained by writing for the college or university newspaper and through a summer internship at a newspaper or other publication. It also may be helpful to submit freelance opinion columns to local or national publications. The more published articles, called "clips," you can show to prospective employers, the better.

Other Requirements

Being a columnist requires similar characteristics to those required for being a reporter: curiosity, a genuine interest in people, the ability to write clearly and succinctly, and the strength to thrive under deadline pressure. But as a columnist, you will also require a certain wit and wisdom, the compunction to express strong opinions, and the ability to take apart an issue and debate it.

EXPLORING

A good way to explore this career is to work for your school newspaper and perhaps write your own column. Participation in debate clubs will help you form opinions and express them clearly. Read your city's newspaper regularly, and take a look at national papers as well as magazines. Which columnists, on the local and national level, interest you? Why do you feel their columns are well done? Try to incorporate these good qualities into your own writing. Contact your local newspaper and ask for a tour of the facilities. This will give you a sense of what the office atmosphere is like and what technologies are used there. Ask to speak with one of the paper's regular columnists about his or her job. He or she may be able to provide you with valuable insights. Visit the Dow Jones Newspaper Fund Web site (http://djnewspaperfund.dowjones.com/fund) for information on careers, summer programs, internships, and more. Try getting a part-time or summer job at the newspaper, even if it's just answering phones and doing data entry. In this way you'll be able to test out how well you like working in such an atmosphere.

EMPLOYERS

Newspapers of all kinds run columns, as do certain magazines and even public radio stations, where a tape is played over the airwaves of the author reading the column. Some columnists are self-employed, preferring to market their work to syndicates instead of working for a single newspaper or magazine.

STARTING OUT

Most columnists start out as reporters. Experienced reporters are the ones most likely to become columnists. Occasionally, however, a relatively new reporter may suggest a weekly column if the beat being covered warrants it, for example, politics.

Another route is to start out by freelancing, sending columns out to a multitude of newspapers and magazines in the hopes that someone will pick them up. Also, columns can be marketed to syndicates. A list of these, and magazines that may also be interested in columns, is provided in the *Writer's Market* (http://www.writers-market.com).

A third possibility, one opened up by the Internet, is simply beginning your own site or blog and using it to attract attention and thus jumpstart your career. Many who are well-known, such as Matt Drudge (http://www.drudgereport.com) and "Wonkette" (http://www.wonkette.com), started by beginning their own Web columns. If you get scoops, run interesting content, and people like what you have to say, you may find yourself with more readers than you can handle.

ADVANCEMENT

Newspaper columnists can advance in national exposure by having their work syndicated. They also may try to get a collection of their columns published in book form. Moving from a small newspaper or magazine to a large national publication is another way to advance.

Columnists also may choose to work in other editorial positions, such as editor, editorial writer or page editor, or foreign correspondent.

EARNINGS

Like reporters' salaries, the incomes of columnists vary greatly according to experience, newspaper size and location, and whether the columnist is under a union contract. But generally, columnists earn higher salaries than reporters.

The U.S. Department of Labor classifies columnists with news analysts, reporters, and correspondents, and reports that the median annual income for these professionals was $32,270 in

2005. Ten percent of those in this group earned less than $18,300, and 10 percent made more than $72,220 annually. According to the *Annual Survey of Journalism & Mass Communication Graduates,* directed by the University of Georgia, the median salary for those who graduated in 2005 with bachelor's degrees in journalism or mass communication was approximately $29,000. Those with master's degrees received average starting salaries of $37,000. Median earnings varied somewhat by employer; for example, those working for weekly papers earned somewhat less, while those working for consumer magazines earned somewhat more. Although these salary figures are for all journalists (not just columnists), they provide a general range for those working in this field. However, popular columnists at large papers earn considerably higher salaries.

Freelancers may get paid by the column. Syndicates pay columnists 40 percent to 60 percent of the sales income generated by their columns or a flat fee if only one column is being sold.

Freelancers must provide their own benefits. Columnists working on staff at newspapers and magazines receive typical benefits such as health insurance, paid vacation days, sick days, and retirement plans.

WORK ENVIRONMENT

Columnists work mostly indoors in newspaper or magazine offices, although they may occasionally conduct interviews or do research on location out of the office. Some columnists may work as much as 48 to 52 hours a week. Some columnists do the majority of their writing at home or in a private office, and come to the newsroom primarily for meetings and to have their work approved or changed by editors. The atmosphere in a newsroom is generally fast paced and loud, so columnists must be able to concentrate and meet deadlines in this type of environment.

OUTLOOK

The U.S. Department of Labor predicts that employment growth for news analysts, reporters, and correspondents (including columnists) will be slower than the average for all occupations through 2014. Growth will be hindered by such factors as mergers and closures of newspapers, decreasing circulation, and lower profits from advertising revenue. Online publications will be a source for new jobs. Competition for newspaper and magazine positions is very competitive, and competition for the position of columnist is even stiffer because

Columnists on the Web

Mitch Albom
http://www.freep.com/index/albom.htm

Maureen Dowd
http://www.nytimes.com/top/opinion/editorialsandoped/oped/
columnists/maureendowd

Matt Drudge
http://www.drudgereport.com

Molly Ivins (deceased)
http://www.creators.com/opinion.html

Mike Lupica
http://www.nydailynews.com/sports/col/lupica/index.html

Robert Novak
http://www.creators.com/opinion.html

Richard Roeper
http://www.suntimes.com/news/roeper/index.html

Neil Steinberg
http://www.suntimes.com/news/steinberg/index.html

Rick Telander
http://www.suntimes.com/sports/telander/index.html

George Will
http://www.washingtonpost.com/wp-dyn/opinion/columns/will-
george

Wonkette (Ana Marie Cox)
http://www.wonkette.com

Fareed Zakaria
http://www.fareedzakaria.com

these are prestigious jobs that are limited in number. Smaller daily and weekly newspapers may be easier places to find employment than major metropolitan newspapers, and movement up the ladder to columnist will also likely be quicker. Pay, however, is less than at bigger papers. Journalism and mass communication graduates will have the best opportunities, and writers will be needed to replace those who leave the field for other work or retire.

FOR MORE INFORMATION

For information on careers in newspaper reporting, education, and financial aid opportunities, contact
American Society of Journalists and Authors
1501 Broadway, Suite 302
New York, NY 10036-5505
Tel: 212-997-0947
http://www.asja.org

This association provides general educational information on all areas of journalism, including newspapers, magazines, television, and radio.
Association for Education in Journalism and Mass Communication
234 Outlet Pointe Boulevard
Columbia, SC 29210-5667
Tel: 803-798-0271
http://www.aejmc.org

For information on a career as a newspaper columnist, contact
National Society of Newspaper Columnists
PO Box 411532
San Francisco, CA 94141-1532
Tel: 866/440-6762
http://www.columnists.com

The SPJ has student chapters all over the United States and offers information on scholarships and internships.
Society of Professional Journalists (SPJ)
3909 North Meridian Street
Indianapolis, IN 46208-4011
Tel: 317-927-8000
http://www.spj.org

Desktop Publishing Specialists

OVERVIEW

Desktop publishing specialists prepare reports, brochures, books, cards, and other documents for printing. They create computer files of text, graphics, and page layout. They work with files others have created, or they compose original text and graphics for clients. There are approximately 34,000 desktop publishing specialists employed in the United States.

HISTORY

When Johannes Gutenberg invented movable type in the 1440s, it was a major technological advancement. Up until that point, books were produced entirely by monks, every word written by hand on vellum. Though print shops flourished all across Europe with this invention, inspiring the production of millions of books by the 1500s, there was little major change in the technology of printing until the 1800s. By then, cylinder presses were churning out thousands of sheets per hour, and the Linotype machine allowed for easier, more efficient plate-making. Offset lithography (a method of applying ink from a treated surface onto paper) followed and gained popularity after World War II. Phototypesetting was later developed, involving creating film images of text and pictures to be printed. At the end of the 20th century, computers caused another revolution in the industry. Laser printers now allow for low-cost, high-quality printing, and desktop publishing software is credited with spurring sales and use of personal home computers.

QUICK FACTS

School Subjects
Art
Computer science
English

Personal Skills
Artistic
Communication/ideas

Work Environment
Primarily indoors
Primarily one location

Minimum Education Level
Some postsecondary training

Salary Range
$19,190 to $32,800 to $53,750+

Certification or Licensing
None available

Outlook
Faster than the average

DOT
979

GOE
01.07.01

NOC
1423

O*NET-SOC
43-9031.00

THE JOB

If you've ever used a computer to design and print a page in your high school paper or yearbook, then you've had some experience in desktop publishing. Not so many years ago, the prepress process (the steps to prepare a document for the printing press) involved metal casts, molten lead, light tables, knives, wax, paste, and a number of different professionals from artists to typesetters. With computer technology, these jobs are becoming more consolidated.

Desktop publishing specialists have artistic talents, proofreading skills, sales and marketing abilities, and a great deal of computer knowledge. They work on computers converting and preparing files for printing presses and other media, such as the Internet and CD-ROM. Much of desktop publishing is called prepress, when specialists typeset, or arrange and transform, text and graphics. They use the latest in design software; programs such as PhotoShop, Illustrator, InDesign (all from software designer Adobe), and QuarkXpress, are the most popular. Some desktop publishing specialists also use CAD (computer-aided design) technology, allowing them to create images and effects with a digitizing pen.

Once they've created a file to be printed, desktop publishing specialists either submit it to a commercial printer or print the pieces themselves. Whereas traditional typesetting costs over $20 per page, desktop printing can cost less than a penny a page. Individuals hire the services of desktop publishing specialists for creating and printing invitations, advertising and fundraising brochures, newsletters, flyers, and business cards. Commercial printing involves catalogs, brochures, and reports, while business printing encompasses products used by businesses, such as sales receipts and forms.

Typesetting and page layout work entails selecting font types and sizes, arranging column widths, checking for proper spacing between letters, words, and columns, placing graphics and pictures, and more. Desktop publishing specialists choose from the hundreds of typefaces available, taking the purpose and tone of the text into consideration when selecting from fonts with round shapes or long shapes, thick strokes or thin, serifs or sans serifs. Editing is also an important duty of a desktop publishing specialist. Articles must be updated, or in some cases rewritten, before they are arranged on a page. As more people use their own desktop publishing programs to create print-ready files, desktop publishing specialists will have to be even more skillful at designing original work and promoting their professional expertise to remain competitive.

Darryl Gabriel and his wife Maree own a desktop publishing service in Australia. The Internet has allowed them to publicize the business globally. They currently serve customers in their local area and across Australia, and are hoping to expand more into international Internet marketing. The Gabriels use a computer ("But one is not enough," Darryl says), a laser printer, and a scanner to create business cards, pamphlets, labels, books, and personalized greeting cards. Though they must maintain computer skills, they also have a practical understanding of the equipment. "We keep our prices down by being able to re-ink our cartridges," Darryl says. "This takes a little getting used to at first, but once you get a knack for it, it becomes easier."

Desktop publishing specialists deal with technical issues, such as resolution problems, colors that need to be corrected, and software difficulties. A client may come in with a hand-drawn sketch, a printout of a design, or a file on a diskette, and he or she may want the piece ready to be posted on the Internet or to be published in a high-quality brochure, newspaper, or magazine. Each format presents different issues, and desktop publishing specialists must be familiar with the processes and solutions for each. They may also provide services such as color scanning, laminating, image manipulation, and poster production.

Customer relations are as important as technical skills. Darryl Gabriel encourages desktop publishing specialists to learn how to use equipment and software to their fullest potential. He also advises them to know their customers. "Try and be as helpful as possible to your customers," he says, "so you can provide them with products that they are happy with and that are going to benefit their businesses." He says it's also very important to follow up, calling customers to make sure they're pleased with the work. "If you're able to relate to what the customers want, and if you encourage them to be involved in the initial design process, then they'll be confident they're going to get quality products."

REQUIREMENTS
High School
Computer classes and design and art classes will help you develop desktop publishing skills. Computer classes should include both hardware and software, since understanding how computers function will help you with troubleshooting and knowing a computer's limits. Through photography classes you can learn about composition, color, and design elements. Typing, drafting, and print shop classes, if available, will also provide you with the opportunity to gain some indispensable skills. Working on the school newspaper or yearbook will train you on desktop publishing skills as well,

including page layout, typesetting, composition, and working under a deadline.

Postsecondary Training

Although a college degree is not a prerequisite, many desktop publishing specialists have at least a bachelor's degree. Areas of study range anywhere from English to graphic design. Some two-year colleges and technical institutes offer programs in desktop publishing or related fields. A growing number of schools offer programs in technical and visual communications, which may include classes in desktop publishing, layout and design, and computer graphics. Four-year colleges also offer courses in technical communications and graphic design. You can enroll in classes related to desktop publishing through extended education programs offered through universities and colleges. These classes, often taught by professionals in the industry, cover basic desktop publishing techniques and advanced lessons on Adobe PhotoShop or QuarkXPress.

Additionally, the Association of Graphic Communications (AGC) offers an Electronic Publishing Certificate program that covers the following topics: electronic publishing introduction, Acrobat and PDF technologies, color theory, graphic design, Illustrator, InDesign, Photoshop, QuarkXPress, prepress and preflight, print production, proofreading and copyediting, electronic publishing, scanning, and typography and font management. Contact the AGC for more information.

Other Requirements

Desktop publishing specialists are detail-oriented, possess problem-solving skills, and have a sense of design and artistic skills. "People tell me I have a flair for graphic design and mixing the right color with the right graphics," Darryl Gabriel says.

A good eye and patience are critical, as well as endurance to see projects through to the finish. You should have an aptitude for computers, the ability to type quickly and accurately, and a natural curiosity. In addition, a calm temperament comes in handy when working under pressure and constant deadlines. You should be flexible and be able to handle more than one project at a time.

EXPLORING

Experimenting with your home computer, or a computer at school or the library, will give you a good idea as to whether desktop publishing is for you. Play around with various graphic design and page layout programs. If you subscribe to an Internet service, take advantage of any free Web space available to you and design your own home page. Join computer clubs and volunteer to produce newsletters and flyers for school or community clubs. Volunteering is an excellent way to try new software and techniques as well as gain experience troubleshooting and creating final products. Part-time or summer employment with printing shops and companies that have in-house publishing or printing departments are other great ways to gain experience and make valuable contacts.

EMPLOYERS

Approximately 34,000 desktop publishing specialists are employed in the United States. Desktop publishing specialists work for individuals and small business owners, such as publishing houses, advertising agencies, graphic design agencies, and printing shops. Some large companies also contract with desktop publishing services rather than hire full-time designers. Government agencies such as the U.S. Government Printing Office hire desktop publishing specialists to help produce the large number of documents they publish.

Desktop publishing specialists deal directly with their clients, but in some cases they may be subcontracting work from printers, designers, and other desktop publishing specialists. They may also work as consultants, working with printing professionals to help solve particular design problems.

STARTING OUT

To start your own business, you must have a great deal of experience with design and page layout, and a careful understanding of the computer design programs you'll be using. Before striking out on your own, you may want to gain experience as a full-time staff member of a large business. Most desktop publishing specialists enter the field through the production side, or the editorial side of the industry. Those with training as a designer or artist can easily master the finer techniques of production. Printing houses and design agencies are places to check for production artist opportunities. Publishing companies often hire desktop publishing specialists to work in-house or as freelance employees. Working within the industry, you can make connections and build up a clientele.

You can also start out by investing in computer hardware and software, and volunteering your services. By designing logos, letterhead, and restaurant menus, for example, your work will gain quick recognition, and word of your services will spread.

ADVANCEMENT

The growth of Darryl and Maree Gabriel's business requires that they invest in another computer and printer. "We want to expand," Darryl says, "and develop with technology by venturing into Internet marketing and development. We also intend to be a thorn in the side of the larger commercial printing businesses in town."

In addition to taking on more print projects, desktop publishing specialists can expand their business into Web design and page layout for Internet-based magazines.

EARNINGS

There is limited salary information available for desktop publishing specialists, most likely because the job duties of desktop publishing specialists can vary and often overlap with other jobs. The average wage of desktop publishing specialists in the prepress department generally ranges from $15 to $50 an hour. Entry-level desktop publishing specialists with little or no experience generally earn minimum wage. Freelancers can earn from $15 to $100 an hour.

According to the U.S. Department of Labor, median annual earnings of desktop publishing specialists were $32,800 in 2005. The lowest 10 percent earned less than $19,190 and the highest 10 percent earned more than $53,750. Wage rates vary depending on experience, training, region, and size of the company.

WORK ENVIRONMENT

Desktop publishing specialists spend most of their time working in front of a computer, whether editing text, or laying out pages. They need to be able to work with other prepress professionals, and deal with clients. Hours may vary depending on project deadlines at hand. Some projects may take just a day to complete, while others may take weeks or months. Projects range from designing a logo for letterhead, to preparing a catalog for the printer, to working on a file for a company's Web site.

OUTLOOK

According to the U.S. Department of Labor, employment for desktop publishing specialists is projected to grow faster than the average for all occupations through 2014, even though overall employment in the printing industry is expected to grow more slowly than the average for all industries. This is due in part because electronic processes are replacing the manual processes performed by paste-up workers, photoengravers, camera operators, film strippers, and platemakers.

As technology advances, the ability to create and publish documents will become easier and faster, thus influencing more businesses to produce printed materials. Desktop publishing specialists will be needed to satisfy typesetting, page layout, design, and editorial demands. With new equipment, commercial printing shops will be able to shorten the turnaround time on projects and in turn can increase business and accept more jobs. For instance, digital printing presses allow printing shops to print directly to the digital press rather than printing to a piece of film, and then printing from the film to the press. Digital printing presses eliminate an entire step and should appeal to companies who need jobs completed quickly.

QuarkXPress, Adobe InDesign, Macromedia FreeHand, Adobe Illustrator, and Adobe PhotoShop are some programs often used in desktop publishing. Specialists with experience in these and other software will be in demand.

FOR MORE INFORMATION

For information on the Electronic Publishing Certificate, contact
Association of Graphic Communications
330 Seventh Avenue, 9th Floor
New York, NY 10001-5010
Tel: 212-279-2100
Email: info@agcomm.org
http://www.agcomm.org

This organization is a source of financial support for education and research projects designed to promote careers in graphic communications. For more information, contact
Graphic Arts Education and Research Foundation
1899 Preston White Drive
Reston, VA 20191-5468
Tel: 866-381-9839
Email: gaerf@npes.org
http://www.gaerf.org

Graphic Arts Information Network
200 Deer Run Road
Sewickley, PA 15143-2324
Tel: 412-741-6860
Email: gain@piagatf.org
http://www.gain.net

National Association for Printing Leadership
75 West Century Road
Paramus, NJ 07652-1408
Tel: 800-642-6275
http://www.recouncil.org

Society for Technical Communication
901 North Stuart Street, Suite 904
Arlington, VA 22203-1822
Tel: 703-522-4114
Email: stc@stc.org
http://www.stc.org

Visit the following Web site for information on scholarships, competitions, colleges and universities that offer graphic communication programs, and careers.
GRAPHIC COMM Central
Email: gcc@teched.vt.edu
http://teched.vt.edu/gcc

Editors

OVERVIEW

Editors perform a wide range of functions, but their primary responsibility is to ensure that text provided by writers is suitable in content, format, and style for the intended audiences. Readers are an editor's first priority. Among the employers of editors are book publishers, magazines, newspapers, newsletters, advertising agencies, radio stations, television stations, Internet sites, and corporations of all kinds. There are about 127,000 editors employed in the United States.

HISTORY

The history of book editing is tied closely to the history of the book and the history of the printing process. The 15th century invention of the printing press by German goldsmith Johannes Gutenberg and the introduction of movable type in the West revolutionized the craft of bookmaking. Books could now be mass-produced. It also became more feasible to make changes to copy before a book was put into production. Printing had been invented hundreds of years earlier in Asia, but books did not proliferate there as quickly as they did in the West, which saw millions of copies in print by 1500.

In the early days of publishing, authors worked directly with the printer, and the printer was often the publisher and seller of the author's work. Eventually, however, booksellers began to work directly with the authors and eventually took over the role of publisher. The publisher then became the middleman between author and printer.

The publisher worked closely with the author and sometimes acted as the editor. The word *editor,* in fact, derives from the Latin

QUICK FACTS

School Subjects
English
Journalism

Personal Interests
Communication/ideas
Helping/teaching

Work Environment
Primarily indoors
Primarily one location

Minimum Education Level
Bachelor's degree

Salary Range
$26,910 to $51,030 to $85,230+

Certification or Licensing
None available

Outlook
About as fast as the average

DOT
132

GOE
01.02.01

NOC
5122

O*NET-SOC
27-3041.00

Paul E. Steiger, managing editor of The Wall Street Journal, discusses the redesign of the newspaper during a press conference. *(Ramon alaie/BloombergNews/Landov)*

word *edere* or *editum* and means supervising or directing the preparation of text. Eventually, specialists were hired to perform the editing function. These editors, who were also called advisors or literary advisors in the 19th century, became an integral part of the publishing business.

The editor, also called the *sponsor* in some houses, sought out the best authors, worked with them, and became their advocate in the publishing house. Some editors became so important that their very presence in a publishing house could determine the quality of authors published there. Some author-editor collaborations have become legendary. The field has grown through the 20th and 21st century, with computers greatly speeding up the editorial process.

THE JOB

Editors work for many kinds of publishers, publications, and corporations. Editors' titles vary widely, not only from one area of publishing to another but also within each area.

Although some editors write for the organizations that employ them, most editors work with material provided by writers. For this reason, one of the most important steps in the editing process is acquiring the work of writers. In the fields of book and journal publishing, that work is usually performed by *acquisitions editors,* who are often called *acquiring editors.* Acquisitions editors may either generate their own ideas or use ideas provided by their publishers or other staff members. If they begin with an idea, they look for writers who can create an effective book or article based on that idea. One benefit of that method is that such ideas are ones that the editors believe are likely to be commercially successful or intellectually successful or both. Often, however, editors use ideas that they receive from writers in the form of proposals.

In some cases, the acquisitions editor will receive a complete manuscript from an author instead of a proposal. Most of the time, however, the writer will submit a query letter that asks whether the editor is interested in a particular idea. If the editor believes that the idea has potential and is suitable for the publishing house, the editor will discuss the idea further with the writer. Unless the writer is well known or is known and trusted by the editor, the editor usually asks the writer for a sample chapter or section. If the editor likes the sample chapter and believes that the author can complete an acceptable manuscript, the publishing house will enter into a contract with the writer. In some cases, the editor will prepare that contract; in others, the contract will be prepared by the publisher or someone else at the publishing house. The contract will specify when the manuscript is due, how much the author will be paid, how long the manuscript must be, and what will happen if the author cannot deliver a manuscript that the editor believes is suitable for publication, among other things.

After the contract has been signed, the writer will begin work. The acquisitions editor must keep track of the author's progress.

Publishing budgets must be prepared in advance so that vendors can be paid and books can be advertised, so it is important that the manuscript be delivered by the due date. Some authors work well on their own and complete their work efficiently and effectively. In many cases, however, authors have problems. They may need advice from the editor regarding content, style, or organization of information. Often, the editor will want to see parts of the manuscript as they are completed. That way, any problems in the writer's work can be identified and solved as soon as possible.

Some typical problems are statements the writer makes that may leave the publisher open to charges of libel or plagiarism. If this problem arises, the editor will require the writer to revise the manuscript. If the writer uses materials that were created by other people (such as long quotations, tables, or artwork), it may be necessary to request permission to use those materials. If permission is required but is not given, the materials cannot be used. It is usually the author's job to obtain permission, but sometimes that task is performed by the editor. In any case, the editor must make sure that necessary permissions are obtained. When an acceptable manuscript has been delivered, the acquisition editor's job is usually complete.

Some publishing houses have editors who specialize in working with authors. These *developmental editors* do not acquire manuscripts. Instead, they make sure the author stays on schedule and does a good job of writing and organizing their material.

Once an acceptable manuscript has been delivered to the publishing house, it is turned over to a *copy editor*. This editor's job is to read the manuscript carefully and make sure that it is sufficiently well written, factually correct (sometimes this job is done by a *researcher* or *fact checker*), grammatically correct, and appropriate in tone and style for its intended readers. Any errors or problems in a printed piece reflect badly not only on the author but also on the publishing house.

The copy editor must be an expert in the English language, have a keen eye for detail, and know how to identify problems. The editor will simply correct some kinds of errors, but in some cases—especially when the piece deals with specialized material—the editor may need to ask, or query, the author about certain points. An editor must never change something that he or she does not understand, since one of the worst errors an editor can make is to change something that is correct to something that is incorrect.

After the copy editor has edited the manuscript, it may be (but is not always) sent to the author for review. When the editor and author have agreed on the final copy, the editor or another specialist will use various kinds of coding to mark the manuscript for typesetting. The codes, which usually correlate to information provided by a graphic designer, tell the typesetter which typefaces to use, how large to make the type, what the layout of the finished pages will look like, and where illustrations or other visual materials will be placed on the pages, among other things.

After the manuscript has been typeset and turned into galley proofs, or typeset copy that has not been divided into pages, the galleys are usually sent to the author to be checked. If the author finds errors or requests that changes be made, the copy editor or the *production editor* will oversee the process, determining which changes will be made.

Managing the editorial staff is the job of the *managing editor,* who draws up budgets for projects, oversees schedules, assigns projects to other editors, and ensures that the editorial staff is working efficiently. The managing editor's boss is the *editor in chief, editorial director,* or *executive editor.* This editor works closely with the publisher, determining the kinds of materials the house will publish and ensuring that the editorial staff carries out the wishes of the publisher. The editor in chief and managing editor also work closely with the heads of other departments, such as marketing, sales, and production.

The basic functions performed by *magazine and newspaper editors* are much like those performed by book editors, but a significant amount of the writing that appears in magazines and newspapers, or periodicals, is done by *staff writers.* Periodicals often use editors who specialize in specific areas, such as *city editors,* who oversee the work of *reporters* who specialize in local news, and department editors. *Department editors* specialize in areas such as business, fashion, sports, and features, to name only a few. These departments are determined by the interests of the audience that the periodical intends to reach. Like book houses, periodicals use copy editors, researchers, and fact checkers, but at small periodicals, one or a few editors may be responsible for tasks that would be performed by many people at a larger publication.

REQUIREMENTS

High School

Editors must be expert communicators, so you should excel in English if you wish to be an editor. You must learn to write extremely well, since you will be correcting and even rewriting the work of others. If elective classes in writing are available in your school, take them. Study journalism and take communications courses. Work as a writer or editor for the school paper. Take a photography class.

Since virtually all editors use computers, take computer courses. You absolutely must learn to type. If you cannot type accurately and rapidly, you will be at an extreme disadvantage. Don't forget, however, that a successful editor must have a wide range of knowledge. The more you know about many areas, the more likely you will be to do well as an editor. Don't hesitate to explore areas that you find interesting. Do everything you can to satisfy your intellectual curiosity. As far as most editors are concerned, there is no useless information.

Postsecondary Training

An editor must have a bachelor's degree, and advanced degrees are highly recommended for book editors and magazine editors. Most editors have degrees in English or journalism, but it is not unheard of for editors to major in one of the other liberal arts. If you know that you want to specialize in a field such as scientific editing, you may wish to major in the area of science of your choice while minoring in English, writing, or journalism. There are many opportunities for editors in technical fields, since most of those who go into editing are interested primarily in the liberal arts. Many colleges offer courses in book editing, magazine design, general editing, and writing. Some colleges, such as the University of Chicago and Stanford University, offer programs in publishing, and many magazines and newspapers offer internships to students. Take advantage of these opportunities. It is extremely important that you gain some practical experience while you are in school. Work on the school paper or find a part-time job with a newspaper or magazine. Don't hesitate to work for a publication in a noneditorial position. The more you know about the publishing business, the better off you will be.

Other Requirements

Good editors are fanatics for the written word. Their passion for good writing comes close to the point of obsession. They are analytical people who know how to think clearly and communicate what they are thinking. They read widely. They not only recognize good English when they see it but also know what makes it good. If they read something they don't understand, they analyze it until they do understand it. If they see a word they don't know, they look it up. When they are curious about something, they research the subject.

You must pay close attention to details to succeed as an editor. You must also be patient, since you may have to spend hours turning a few pages of near-gibberish into powerful, elegant English. If you are the kind of person who can't sit still, you probably will not succeed as an editor. To be a good editor, you must be a self-starter who is not afraid to make decisions. You must be good not only at identifying problems but also at solving them, so you must be creative. If you are both creative and a perfectionist, editing may be the line of work for you.

EXPLORING

One of the best ways to explore the field of editing is to work on a school newspaper or other publication. The experience you gain will definitely be helpful, even if your duties are not strictly editorial. Being involved in writing, reporting, typesetting, proofreading, printing, or any other task will help you to understand editing and how it relates to the entire field of publishing.

If you cannot work for the school paper, try to land a part-time job with a local newspaper or newsletter, or publish your own newsletter. You may try combining another interest with your interest in editing. For example, if you are interested in environmental issues, you might want to start a newsletter that deals with environmental problems and solutions in your community.

Another useful project is keeping a journal. In fact, any writing project will be helpful, since editing and writing are inextricably linked. Write something every day. Try to rework your writing until it is as good as you can make it. Try different kinds of writing, such as letters to the editor, short stories, poetry, essays, comedic prose, and plays.

The American Copy Editors Society offers a wide variety of resources for aspiring and professional copy editors at its Web site (http://www.copydesk.org). These include articles about copyediting, a discussion board, a practice copyediting test, and suggested books and Web sites. The society also offers membership to high school students who are taking journalism courses or working on a school or alternative publication.

EMPLOYERS

Approximately 127,000 editors are employed in the United States. One of the best things about the field of editing is that there are many kinds of opportunities for editors. The most obvious employers for editors are book publishers, magazines, and newspapers. There are many varieties of all three of these types of publishers. There are small and large publishers, general and specialized publishers, local and national publishers. If you have a strong interest in a particular field, you will undoubtedly find various publishers that specialize in it.

Another excellent source of employment is business. Almost all businesses of any size need writers and editors on a full-time or part-time basis. Corporations often publish newsletters for their employees or produce publications that talk about how they do business. Large companies produce annual reports that must be written and edited. In addition, advertising is a major source of work for editors, proofreaders, and writers. Advertising agencies use editors, proofreaders, and quality-control people, as do typesetting and printing companies (in many cases, proofreaders edit as well as proofread). Keep in mind that somebody has to work on all the printed material you see every day, from books and magazines to menus and matchbooks.

STARTING OUT

There is tremendous competition for editorial jobs, so it is important for a beginner who wishes to break into the business to be as well prepared as possible. College students who have gained experience as interns, have worked for publications during the summers, or have attended special programs in publishing will be at an advantage. In addition, applicants for any editorial position must be extremely careful when preparing cover letters and resumes. Even a single error in spelling or usage will disqualify an applicant. Applicants for editorial or proofreading positions must also expect to take and pass tests that are designed to determine their language skills.

Many editors enter the field as editorial assistants or proofreaders. Some editorial assistants perform only clerical tasks, whereas others may also proofread or perform basic editorial tasks. Typically, an editorial assistant who performs well will be given the opportunity to take on more and more editorial duties. Proofreaders have the advantage of being able to look at the work of editors, so they can learn while they do their own work.

Good sources of information about job openings are school career services offices, classified ads in newspapers and trade journals, specialized publications such as *Publishers Weekly* (http://publishersweekly.com), and Internet sites. One way to proceed is to identify local publishers through the Yellow Pages. Many publishers have Web sites that list job openings, and large publishers often have telephone job lines that serve the same purpose.

ADVANCEMENT

In book houses, employees who start as editorial assistants or proofreaders and show promise generally become copy editors. After gaining skill in that position, they may be given a wider range of duties while retaining the same title. The next step may be a position as a *senior copy editor,* which involves overseeing the work of junior copy editors, or as a *project editor.* The project editor performs a wide variety of tasks, including copyediting, coordinating the work of in-house and freelance copy editors, and managing the schedule of a particular project. From this position, an editor may move up to become assistant editor, then managing editor, then editor in chief. These positions involve more management and decision making than is usually found in the positions described previously. The editor in chief works with the publisher to ensure that a suitable editorial policy is being followed, while the managing editor is responsible for all aspects of the editorial department. The *assistant editor* provides support to the managing editor. (It should be noted that job titles and responsibilities can vary from publishing house to publishing house.)

Newspaper editors generally begin working on the copy desk, where they progress from less significant stories and projects to major news and feature stories. A common route to advancement is for copy editors to be promoted to a particular department, where they may move up the ranks to management positions. An editor who has achieved success in a department may become a city editor, who is responsible for news, or a managing editor, who runs the entire editorial operation of a newspaper.

Magazine editors advance in much the same way that book editors do. After they become copy editors, they work their way up to become senior editors, managing editors, and editors-in-chief. In many cases, magazine editors advance by moving from a position on one magazine to the same position with a larger or more prestigious magazine. Such moves often bring significant increases in both pay and status.

EARNINGS

Although a small percentage of editors are paid extremely well, the average editor is not well paid. Competition for editing jobs is fierce, and there is no shortage of people who wish to enter the field. For that reason, companies that employ editors generally pay relatively low wages.

According to 2005 data from the U.S. Department of Labor, mean annual earnings for editors employed in newspaper, book, and directory publishing were $45,510. The lowest 10 percent earned less than $26,910 and the highest 10 percent earned more than $85,230.

Technical editors usually make more money than newspaper, magazine, or book editors. According to a 2005 salary survey conducted by the Society for Technical Communication, the average salary for technical writers and editors was $67,520.

WORK ENVIRONMENT

The environments in which editors work vary widely. For the most part, publishers of all kinds realize that a quiet atmosphere is conducive to work that requires tremendous concentration. It takes an unusual ability to focus to edit in a noisy place. Most editors work in private offices or cubicles. Book editors often work in quieter surroundings than do newspaper editors or quality-control people in advertising agencies, who sometimes work in rather loud and hectic situations.

Even in relatively quiet surroundings, however, editors often have many distractions. A project editor who is trying to do some copyediting or review the editing of others may, for example, have to deal with phone calls from authors, questions from junior editors, meetings with members of the editorial and production staff, and questions from freelancers, among many other distractions. In many cases, editors have computers that are exclusively for their own use, but in others, editors must share computers that are located in a common area.

Deadlines are an important issue for virtually all editors. Newspaper and magazine editors work in a much more pressurized atmosphere than book editors because they face daily or weekly deadlines, whereas book production usually takes place over several months.

In almost all cases, editors must work long hours during certain phases of the editing process. Some newspaper editors start work at 5:00 A.M., others work until 11:00 P.M. or even through the night. Feature editors, columnists, and editorial page editors usually can schedule their day in a more regular fashion, as can editors who work on weekly newspapers. Editors working on hard news, however, may receive an assignment that must be completed, even if work extends well into the next shift.

OUTLOOK

According to the *Occupational Outlook Handbook,* employment of editors will increase about as fast as the average for all occupations through 2014. Competition for those jobs will remain intense, since so many people want to enter the field. Book publishing will remain particularly competitive, since many people still view the field in a romantic light.

One of the major trends in publishing is specialization. More and more publishing ventures are targeting relatively narrow markets, which means that there are more opportunities for editors to combine their work and their personal interests. It is also true, however, that many of these specialty publications do not survive for long.

There will be increasing job opportunities for editors in Internet publishing as online publishing and services continue to grow. Advertising and public relations will also provide employment opportunities.

A fairly large number of positions—both fulltime and freelance—become available when experienced editors leave the business for other fields. Many editors make this decision because they find that they can make more money in other businesses than they can as editors.

FOR MORE INFORMATION

The following organization's Web site is an excellent source of information about careers in editing. The ACES organizes educational seminars and maintains lists of internships.
American Copy Editors Society (ACES)
Three Healy Street
Huntington, NY 11743-5323
http://www.copydesk.org

The ASNE helps editors maintain the highest standards of quality, improve their craft, and better serve their communities. It preserves and promotes core journalistic values. Visit its Web site to read online publications such as Why Choose Journalism? *and* Preparing for a Career in Newspapers.
American Society of Newspaper Editors (ASNE)
11690B Sunrise Valley Drive
Reston, VA 20191-1409
Tel: 703-453-1122
Email: asne@asne.org
http://www.asne.org

This organization of book publishers offers an extensive Web site about the book business.
Association of American Publishers
71 Fifth Avenue, Second Floor
New York, NY 10003-3004
Tel: 212-255-0200

Email: info@bookjobs.org
http://www.publishers.org

This organization provides information about internships and about the newspaper business in general.
Dow Jones Newspaper Fund
PO Box 300
Princeton, NJ 08543-0300
Tel: 609-452-2820
Email: newsfund@wsj.dowjones.com
http://djnewspaperfund.dowjones.com/fund

The EFA is an organization for freelance editors. Members receive a newsletter and a free listing in their directory.
Editorial Freelancers Association (EFA)
71 West 23rd Street, Suite 1910
New York, NY 10010-4181
Tel: 866-929-5400
Email: info@the-efa.org
http://www.the-efa.org

This organization is a good source of information on internships.
Magazine Publishers of America
810 Seventh Avenue, 24th Floor
New York, NY 10019-5873
Tel: 212-872-3700
Email: mpa@magazine.org
http://www.magazine.org

For information on careers, contact
Society for Technical Communication
901 North Stuart Street, Suite 904
Arlington, VA 22203-1822
Tel: 703-522-4114
Email: stc@stc.org
http://www.stc.org

The Slot is a Web site founded and maintained by Bill Walsh, national copy desk chief at The Washington Post. Walsh's tips on proper word usage, grammar lessons, and style guides are both informative and funny.
The Slot
http://www.theslot.com

Graphic Designers

OVERVIEW

Graphic designers are practical artists whose creations are intended to express ideas, convey information, or draw attention to a product. They design a wide variety of materials including advertisements, displays, packaging, signs, computer graphics and games, book and magazine covers and interiors, animated characters, and company logos to fit the needs and preferences of their various clients. There are approximately 228,000 graphic designers employed in the United States.

HISTORY

The challenge of combining beauty, function, and technology in whatever form has preoccupied artisans throughout history. Graphic design work has been used to create products and promote commerce for as long as people have used symbols, pictures, and typography to communicate ideas.

Graphic design grew alongside the growth of print media (newspapers, magazines, catalogs, and advertising). Typically, the graphic designer would sketch several rough drafts of the layout of pictures and words. After one of the drafts was approved, the designer would complete a final layout including detailed type and artwork specifications. The words were sent to a typesetter and the artwork assigned to an illustrator. When the final pieces were returned, the designer or a keyline and paste-up artist would adhere them with rubber cement or wax to an illustration board. Different colored items were placed on acetate overlays. This camera-ready art was now ready to be sent to a printer for photographing and reproduction.

QUICK FACTS

School Subjects
Art
Computer science

Personal Skills
Artistic
Communication/ideas

Work Environment
Primarily indoors
Primarily one location

Minimum Education Level
Some postsecondary training

Salary Range
$23,160 to $38,390 to
$110,000+

Certification or Licensing
None available

Outlook
About as fast as the average

DOT
141

GOE
01.04.02

NOC
5241

O*NET-SOC
27-1024.00

Computer technology has revolutionized the way many graphic designers do their work. Today it is possible to be a successful graphic designer even if you can't draw more than simple stick figures. Graphic designers are now able to draw, color, and revise the many different images they work with using computers. They can choose typefaces, size type, and place images without having to manually align them on the page using a T square and triangle. Computer graphics enable graphic designers to work more quickly, since details like size, shape, and color are easy to change.

Graphics design programs are continually revised and improved, moving more and more design work from the artist's table to the computer mouse pad and graphics tablet. As computer technology continues to advance in the areas of graphics and multimedia, more designers will have to know how to work with virtual reality applications.

THE JOB

Graphic designers are not primarily fine artists, although they may be highly skilled at drawing or painting. Most designs commissioned to graphic designers involve both artwork and copy (words). Thus, the designer must not only be familiar with the wide range of art media (photography, drawing, painting, collage, etc.) and styles, but he or she must also be familiar with a wide range of typefaces and know how to manipulate them for the right effect. Because design tends to change in a similar way to fashion, designers must keep up to date with the latest trends. At the same time, they must be well grounded in more traditional, classic designs.

Graphic designers can work as *in-house designers* for a particular company, as *staff designers* for a graphic design firm, or as *freelance designers* working for themselves. Some designers specialize in designing advertising materials or packaging. Others focus on corporate identity materials such as company stationery and logos. Some work mainly for publishers, designing book and magazine covers and page layouts. Some work in the area of computer graphics, creating still or animated graphics for computer software, videos, or motion pictures. A highly specialized type of graphic designer, the *environmental graphic designer,* designs large outdoor signs. Depending on the project's requirements, some graphic designers work exclusively on the computer, while others may use both the computer and drawings or paintings created by hand.

Whatever the specialty and whatever their medium, all graphic designers take a similar approach to a project, whether it is for an entirely new design or for a variation on an existing one. Graphic designers begin by determining the needs and preferences of clients and potential users, buyers, or viewers.

For example, if a graphic designer is working on a company logo, he or she will likely meet with company representatives to discuss such points as how and where the company is going to use the logo and what size, color, and shape preferences company executives might have. Project budgets must be respected: A design that may be perfect in every way but that is too costly to reproduce is basically useless. Graphic designers may need to compare their ideas with similar ones from other companies and analyze the image they project. They must have a good knowledge of how various colors, shapes, and layouts affect the viewer psychologically.

After a plan has been conceived and the details worked out, the graphic designer does some preliminary designs (generally two or three) to present to the client for approval. The client may reject the preliminary designs entirely and request a new one, or he or she may ask the designer to make alterations. The designer then goes back to the drawing board to attempt a new design or make the requested changes. This process continues until the client approves the design.

Once a design has been approved, the graphic designer prepares the piece for professional reproduction, or printing. The printer may require what is called a mechanical, in which the artwork and copy are arranged on a white board just as it is to be photographed, or the designer may be asked to submit an electronic copy of the design. Either way, designers must have a good understanding of the printing process, including color separation, paper properties, and halftone (photograph) reproduction.

REQUIREMENTS

High School
While in high school, take any art and design courses that are available. Computer classes are also helpful, particularly those that teach page layout programs or art and photography manipulation programs. Working on the school newspaper or yearbook can provide valuable design experience. You could also volunteer to design flyers or posters for school events.

Postsecondary Training
More graphic designers are recognizing the value of formal training; at least two out of three people entering the field today have a college degree or some college education. About 250 colleges and art schools offer art and graphic design programs that

are accredited by the National Association of Schools of Art and Design. At many schools, graphic design students must take a year of basic art and design courses before being accepted into the bachelor's degree program. In addition, applicants to the bachelor's degree programs in graphic arts may be asked to submit samples of their work to prove artistic ability. Many schools and employers depend on samples, or portfolios, to evaluate the applicants' skills in graphic design.

Many programs increasingly emphasize the importance of using computers for design work. Computer proficiency will be very important in the years to come. Interested individuals should select an academic program that incorporates computer training into the curriculum, or train themselves on their own.

A bachelor of fine arts program at a four-year college or university may include courses such as principles of design, art and art history, painting, sculpture, mechanical and architectural drawing, architecture, computer design, basic engineering, fashion designing and sketching, garment construction, and textiles. Such degrees are desirable but not always necessary for obtaining a position as a graphic designer.

Other Requirements

As with all artists, graphic designers need a degree of artistic talent, creativity, and imagination. They must be sensitive to beauty, have an eye for detail, and have a strong sense of color, balance, and proportion. Much of these qualities come naturally to potential graphic designers, but skills can be developed and improved through training, both on the job and in professional schools, colleges, and universities.

More and more graphic designers need solid computer skills and working knowledge of several of the common drawing, image editing, and page layout programs. Graphic design can be done on both Macintosh systems and on PCs; in fact, many designers have both types of computers in their studios.

With or without specialized education, graphic designers seeking employment should have a good portfolio containing samples of their best work. The graphic designer's portfolio is extremely important and can make a difference when an employer must choose between two otherwise equally qualified candidates.

A period of on-the-job training is expected for all beginning designers. The length of time it takes to become fully qualified as a graphic designer may run from one to three years, depending on prior education and experience, as well as innate talent.

EXPLORING

If you are interested in a career in graphic design, there are a number of ways to find out whether you have the talent, ambition, and perseverance to succeed in the field. Take as many art and design courses as possible while still in high school and become proficient at working on computers. To get an insider's view of various design occupations, you could enlist the help of art teachers or school guidance counselors to make arrangements to tour design firms and interview designers.

While in school, seek out practical experience by participating in school and community projects that call for design talents. These might include such activities as building sets for plays, setting up exhibits, planning seasonal and holiday displays, and preparing programs and other printed materials. If you are interested in publication design, work on the school newspaper or yearbook is invaluable.

Part-time and summer jobs are excellent ways to become familiar with the day-to-day requirements of a design job and gain some basic related experience. Possible places of employment include design studios, design departments in advertising agencies and manufacturing companies, department and furniture stores, flower shops, workshops that produce ornamental items, and museums. Museums also use a number of volunteer workers. Inexperienced people are often employed as sales, clerical, or general assistants; those with a little more education and experience may qualify for jobs in which they have a chance to develop actual design skills and build portfolios of completed design projects.

EMPLOYERS

Graphic designers hold approximately 228,000 jobs. They work in many different industries, including the wholesale and retail trade (such as department stores, furniture and home furnishings stores, apparel stores, and florist shops); manufacturing industries (such as machinery, motor vehicles, aircraft, metal products, instruments, apparel, textiles, printing, and publishing); service industries (such as business services, engineering, and architecture); construction firms; and government agencies. Public relations and publicity firms, advertising agencies, and mail-order houses all have graphic design departments. The publishing industry is a primary employer of graphic designers, including book publishers, magazines, newspapers, and newsletters.

About 30 percent of all graphic designers are self-employed, a higher proportion than is found in most other occupations. These freelance designers sell their services to multiple clients.

STARTING OUT

The best way to enter the field of graphic design is to have a strong portfolio. Potential employers rely on portfolios to evaluate talent and how that talent might be used to fit the company's needs. Beginning graphic designers can assemble a portfolio from work completed at school, in art classes, and in part-time or freelance jobs. The portfolio should continually be updated to reflect the designer's growing skills so it will always be ready for possible job changes.

Those just starting out can apply directly to companies that employ designers. Many colleges and professional schools have placement services to help graduates find positions, and sometimes it is possible to get a referral from a previous part-time employer or volunteer coordinator.

ADVANCEMENT

As part of their on-the-job training, beginning graphic designers generally are given simpler tasks and work under direct supervision. As they gain experience, they move up to more complex work with increasingly less supervision. Experienced graphic designers, especially those with leadership capabilities, may be promoted to chief designer, design department head, or other supervisory positions.

Graphic designers with strong computer skills can move into other computer-related positions with additional education. Some may become interested in graphics programming in order to further improve computer design capabilities. Others may want to become involved with multimedia and interactive graphics. Video games, touch-screen displays in stores, and even laser light shows are all products of multimedia graphic designers.

When designers develop personal styles that are in high demand in the marketplace, they sometimes go into business for themselves. Freelance design work can be erratic, however, so usually only the most experienced designers with an established client base can count on consistent full-time work.

EARNINGS

The range of salaries for graphic designers is quite broad. Many earn as little as $20,000, while others make more than $110,000.

Books to Read

Bruno, Michael H. (ed.) *Pocket Pal: A Graphic Arts Production Handbook*. 18th ed. Sewickley, Pa.: Graphic Arts Technical Foundation, 2000.

Campbell, Alastair. *The Designer's Lexicon: The Illustrated Dictionary of Design, Printing, and Computer Terms*. San Francisco, Calif. Chronicle Books, 2000.

Cox, Mary (ed.). *Artist's & Graphic Designer's Market 2007*. Cincinnati, Ohio: Writers Digest Books, 2006.

Hollis, Richard. *Graphic Design: A Concise History*. 2d ed. London: Thames & Hudson, 2002.

Lupton, Ellen. *Thinking with Type: A Critical Guide for Designers, Writers, Editors, & Students*. New York: Princeton Architectural Press, 2004.

Parker, Roger C. *Looking Good in Print*. 6th ed. Phoenix, Ariz.: Paraglyph Press, 2006.

Shaughnessy, Adrian, and Stefan Sagmeister. *How To Be a Graphic Designer Without Losing Your Soul*. New York: Princeton Architectural Press, 2005.

Williams, Robin. *The Non-Designer's Design Book*. 2d ed. Berkeley, Calif.: Peachpit Press, 2003.

Williams, Robin, and John Tollett. *Robin Williams Design Workshop*. 2d ed. Berkeley, Calif.: Peachpit Press, 2006.

Salaries depend primarily on the nature and scope of the employer. The U.S. Department of Labor reports that in 2005, graphic designers employed in newspaper, book, and directory publishing earned a mean salary of $36,850; the highest paid 10 percent of all graphic designers earned $67,660 or more, while the lowest paid 10 percent earned $23,160 or less.

The American Institute of Graphic Arts/Aquent Salary Survey 2005 reports that designers earned a median salary of $42,500 in 2005, while senior designers earned a median of $56,000 annually. Salaried designers who advance to the position of creative/design director earned a median of $90,000 a year. The owner of a consulting firm can make $105,000.

Self-employed designers can earn a lot one year and substantially more or less the next. Their earnings depend on individual talent and business ability, but, in general, are higher than those of salaried designers. Although like any self-employed individual, freelance designers must pay their own insurance costs and taxes and are not compensated for vacation or sick days.

Graphic designers who work for large corporations receive full benefits, including health insurance, paid vacation, and sick leave.

WORK ENVIRONMENT

Most graphic designers work regular hours in clean, comfortable, pleasant offices or studios. Conditions vary depending on the design specialty. Some graphic designers work in small establishments with few employees; others work in large organizations with large design departments. Some deal mostly with their coworkers; others may have a lot of public contact. Freelance designers are paid by the assignment. To maintain a steady income, they must constantly strive to please their clients and to find new ones. At times, graphic designers may have to work long, irregular hours in order to complete an especially ambitious project.

OUTLOOK

Employment for qualified graphic designers is expected to grow about as fast as the average for all occupations through 2014; employment should be especially strong for those involved with computer graphics and animation. As computer graphic and Web-based technology continues to advance, there will be a need for well-trained computer graphic designers. Companies that have always used graphic designers will expect their designers to perform work on computers. Companies for which graphic design was once too time consuming or costly are now sprucing up company newsletters and magazines, among other things, requiring the skills of design professionals.

Because the design field appeals to many talented individuals, competition is expected to be strong in all areas. Beginners and designers with only average talent or without formal education and technical skills may encounter some difficulty in finding a job.

FOR MORE INFORMATION

For more information about careers in graphic design, contact
American Institute of Graphic Arts
164 Fifth Avenue
New York, NY 10010-5901
Tel: 212-807-1990
http://www.aiga.org

Visit the NASAD's Web site for information on schools.
National Association of Schools of Art and Design (NASAD)
11250 Roger Bacon Drive, Suite 21
Reston, VA 20190-5248
Tel: 703-437-0700
Email: info@arts-accredit.org
http://nasad.arts-accredit.org

To read an online newsletter featuring competitions, examples of top designers' work, and industry news, visit the SPD's Web site.
Society of Publication Designers (SPD)
17 East 47th Street, 6th Floor
New York, NY 10017-1920
Tel: 212-223-3332
Email: mail@spd.org
http://www.spd.org

Indexers

OVERVIEW

Indexers compile organized lists, called indexes, that help people locate information in a text or body of work. Indexes are like "road maps" that help users find desired information. Just as a map allows travelers to select the most direct route to a destination, indexes should provide users with a basis for selecting relevant information and screening out that which is unwanted.

HISTORY

The first known finding list was compiled by Callimachus, a Greek poet and scholar of the third century B.C., to provide a guide to the contents of the Alexandrian Library. Primitive alphabetical indexes began to appear in the 16th century A.D. In 1614, the bishop of Petina, Antonio Zara, included an index in his *Anatomia ingeniorum etscientiarum (Anatomy of Talents and Sciences),* and in 1677, Johann Jacob Hoffman added an index to his *Lexicon universale.* These early indexes were difficult to use because entries under each letter of the alphabet were not arranged alphabetically. Every term beginning with a "B" would appear somewhere under that letter, but subjects beginning "Ba" did not necessarily precede those beginning "Be."

In the 18th century, alphabetic indexing improved, as demonstrated in Denis Diderot's *Encyclopedie,* which is alphabetized consistently throughout. In the 19th century, indexers attempted to compile indexes that covered entire fields of knowledge. The *Reader's Guide to Periodic Literature,* published by H.W. Wilson Company of New York, is one of the best-known examples of an index that includes references to many publications.

The 20th century revolutionized the fields of indexing and information retrieval by introducing computer technology. There are now many computer programs designed to assist in the preparation of indexes. Some programs, in fact, have largely automated the mechanical aspects of indexing.

THE JOB

There are several types of common indexes. The most familiar is the back-of-book index. Back-of-book indexes contain references to information in only one volume. Most nonfiction, single-volume texts include this sort of index. Multivolume indexes contain references to information in more than one volume. The page references in a multivolume index must indicate clearly both the volume number and the page number of the cited information. Most encyclopedias include multivolume indexes. Magazines and newspapers also have indexes. These periodical indexes are published separately, at regular intervals throughout the year, and are extremely helpful to researchers.

A more recent development in indexing is the online index. Online indexes help users locate specific information from within a large database. Online indexes differ from a simple search function in that an indexer has created a translational thesaurus. When a user inputs a term that actually does not exist in the database, the online index will translate the term to a synonym that does exist so that the user may access the needed information.

Though their scope and purposes vary widely, all indexes have certain features in common. Every index must be organized according to a useful system. Most indexes are alphabetical, though in some specialized cases they may be chronological or numerical. The index to a history text, for instance, might be in chronological order. The two most commonly used alphabetical filing systems are the word-by-word arrangement, under which New York would precede Newark, and the letter-by-letter arrangement, under which New York would follow Newark.

All indexes must contain index terms, called headings, and page numbers or other locators. Most indexes also contain subheadings that help users narrow their search for information. Under the main heading "George Washington," for example, an indexer might use subheadings to separate references to the Revolutionary War from those to Washington's presidency. An index also may include cross-references to other pertinent headings or indicate the presence of illustrations, charts, and bibliographies.

Whether one creates an index on three-by-five index cards or with the help of a software program, the mental process is the same. The indexer first must read and understand the primary information in the text. Only then can the indexer begin to identify key terms and concepts. The second phase in compiling an index is called tracing—marking terms or concepts. Choosing appropriate headings is often the most challenging aspect of an indexer's job. Subjects must be indexed not only under the terms used in the text, but also under the terms that may occur to the reader. Since the indexer's first obligation is to help the reader find information, the best indexers ask themselves, "Where would the reader look?"

After tracing, the indexer begins to compile the headings and page references. Entries with many page citations must be divided further by subheadings. The final step in creating an index is editing. The indexer must view the index as a whole in order to polish the organization, delete trivial references, and add appropriate subheadings.

While indexers may organize information by key words or concepts, the most useful indexes usually combine both systems. Key word compilation is indiscriminate and is of limited usefulness to the reader. Key word lists include every instance of a term and usually fail to make connections between synonymous or related terms. Computer programs that promise automated indexing are actually capable only of compiling such key word concordances. In conceptual indexing, on the other hand, the indexer is not bound to standardized terminology, but recognizes synonymous or related information and disregards trivial references. Even the most sophisticated computer program is incapable of creating an adequate conceptual index.

REQUIREMENTS

High School

Although there is no one educational path that best prepares students to become indexers, a high school diploma and a college degree are necessary. Classes in English and computers are essential, and classes in history and other social sciences will familiarize you with a broad range of subjects that might be indexed.

Postsecondary Training

Since indexers must be well-read and knowledgeable about a wide range of academic disciplines, a liberal arts degree is highly recommended. Many indexers have one or more advanced degrees as well. Professional training is not required but can be extremely helpful. Though few educational institutions offer indexing courses, many offer relevant classes that may be useful to indexers, such as Information Storage and Retrieval, Introduction to Information Science, and Cataloging and Classification. Additionally, correspondence courses in indexing are available through the Graduate School, U.S. Department of Agriculture (http://www.grad.usda.gov). The American Society of Indexers also offers an online training course in indexing. Those who complete three self-study units (Indexers, Users, and Documents; Choice and Form of Entries; and Arrangement and Presentation of Indexes and Thesauri) and pass an examination for each unit receive a certificate of completion in indexing training. For more information, visit http://www.asindexing.org/site/certfaq.shtml.

Today's indexers must be computer literate to be competitive. Manual preparation of indexes is a dying art due to the widespread availability of computer programs designed to automate the mechanics of indexing. This trend toward computer-assisted indexing will continue as more and more information is created and stored in electronic format. Tomorrow's indexers will often create online indexes for large databases rather than the familiar back-of-book variety. With the incredible proliferation of information in the late 20th and early 21st century, information management has become an increasingly complex and competitive field. Those who would be indexers must be prepared to adapt rapidly as methods of storing and disseminating information continue to change and advance in the next decade. With this in mind, aspiring indexers would do well to pursue degrees in library or information science.

Other Requirements

Indexing can be an extremely solitary profession. Indexers should enjoy intellectual challenges and have a passion for coherent structure. To be successful, indexers must also have great patience for detail.

EXPLORING

To explore the indexing profession, interested high school students should visit libraries to read and evaluate indexes of all kinds. Students also should read some basic books on the practice and theory of indexing, such as *Indexing Books* (Chicago: University of Chicago Press, 2005); *Indexing from A to Z* (New York: H.W. Wilson, 1996); or *Handbook of Indexing Techniques: A Guide for Beginning Indexers* (Corpus Christi, Texas: Fetters InfoManagement Co., 2001). The American Society of Indexers publishes several helpful pamphlets on getting started in the indexing profession.

EMPLOYERS

Traditionally, indexers have worked for publishers of books or periodicals. Publishers of encyclopedias, legal books, and newspapers usually employ a staff of indexers. They are full-time employees, or they earn a living by freelance indexing. Freelance indexers are self-employed workers who sell their indexing services. Publishers hire freelance indexers to work on specific books or projects.

STARTING OUT

Novice indexers can enter the field by becoming a junior member of an indexing team at a large publishing house. Beginners commonly work under the close supervision of a more experienced staff member. Freelance indexers begin by soliciting work—a time-consuming and difficult process. In order to gain experience and build client relationships, novice indexers must initially accept small jobs at relatively low pay rates.

ADVANCEMENT

Junior indexers may advance to positions of greater seniority in two to three years. Eventually, an indexer can attain a supervisory position within an indexing department. Experienced freelance indexers may charge reasonably higher rates as their level of expertise increases.

EARNINGS

The average salary for a beginning indexer is about $20,000. More experienced indexers can earn $25,000 to $30,000 as they acquire more supervisory responsibilities and seniority. Freelance indexing has the potential to be more lucrative than in-house indexing, but offers less financial security. Freelance indexers must provide their own offices, equipment, and health insurance. In general, hourly rates more accurately reflect the indexer's efforts than per entry or per page rates because indexes that involve extensive conceptual work may have relatively few entries. Freelance indexers can earn from $20,000 to $70,000 annually, depending on their level of experience.

WORK ENVIRONMENT

Full-time indexers usually work between 35 and 40 hours a week in typical office settings. Freelance indexers may work out of their homes or take temporary assignments in the offices of employers. The amount of pressure an indexer experiences varies greatly with the type of indexing. Those who compile indexes for newspapers must sift rapidly through great quantities of information and regularly work long hours. Encyclopedia indexers, on the other hand, may face deadlines only once a year. Freelance indexers have irregular schedules; a freelance indexer may work extremely long hours when completing several projects at once but have relatively little work the following week. In general, freelance indexing is more stressful than in-house work as freelancers must constantly plan out their own work schedules, send invoices, and keep business records, in addition to indexing.

OUTLOOK

Publishers in the 21st century will tend toward computer-assisted indexing, making it necessary for indexers to be well versed in the use of computer programs. Computers are not likely to replace human indexers, who have thought-processing abilities, anytime soon. Publishers of reference material, newspapers, and scholarly works will continue to value competent indexers. In addition, as information replaces manufacturing as the world's most valuable industry, new opportunities for indexers should become available.

FOR MORE INFORMATION

For information on careers in indexing, contact
American Society of Indexers
10200 West 44th Avenue, Suite 304
Wheat Ridge, CO 80033-2840
Tel: 303-463-2887
Email: info@asindexing.org
http://www.asindexing.org

For information on home-study courses in indexing, contact
Correspondence Study Program
Graduate School, USDA
600 Maryland Avenue, SW, Suite 120
Washington, DC 20024-2520
Tel: 888-744-4723
Email: customerservicecenter@grad.usda.gov
http://www.grad.usda.gov

INTERVIEW

Donald Glassman is the owner of Glassman Indexing Services in Ankeny, Iowa. He discussed his career with the editors of Careers in Focus: Publishing.

Q. Please tell us about yourself and your business.

A. I have a B.S. in zoology, an M.S. in microbiology, and a D.V.M. in veterinary medicine. I was a full-time practicing veterinarian for almost 10 years when I experienced a bit of a burn-out and was looking for something fresh and challenging to do with my career. I happened to read an article in *Money* magazine about a guy who indexed for a career and seemed to make good money. I had no idea that there was such a thing as an "indexer" until I saw that article. I love books, I love to read, I am tremendously organized and meticulous; indexing seemed like an incredible match for me.

It is now 10 years later, and I have built a very nice career for myself as a freelance indexer. I index between 45 and 60 books a year from the comfort of my home. I have about a dozen publishers that send work to me on a regular basis. My income fluctuates throughout the year, but has increased every year that I have been in business. I like the fact that the harder I work the more income I earn. I create indexes for both books and scientific journals. Because of my extensive science background, I tend to index many science books, but I love variety and index histories, travel books, exercise books, home-improvement books, gardening books, and a wide range of other subjects.

Q. How did you train for this job? What was your college major or did you train in another way?

A. I trained by taking an indexing correspondence course from the U.S. Department of Agriculture graduate school. The American Society of Indexers has just started a course for aspiring indexers. I also consider myself to be predominately self-taught. To see if I had what it took to be an indexer, I went to a bookstore and bought five smallish books which contained indexes. I removed the indexes from the books and created my own indexes for each book. When I compared my indexes to the published indexes for the books and found mine were pretty darn good, I knew I could make it as an indexer.

Quite a few indexers have degrees in library science, but there are many more who have a wide range of degrees.

Q. What are the most important qualities for indexers?

A. An indexer must be a very organized, structured thinker. Responsibility and dependability are also a must. The publishing of a book is often on a very tight schedule and an index absolutely can't be late in getting to the publisher. Although some indexers work on-site for publishing houses, most are freelancers working from home, so an indexer must enjoy working alone. Oh, and you gotta love books!

Q. What activities would you suggest to high school students who are interested in this career?

A. If a student has an interest in indexing they might try something like I did and attempt to create their own index for a book chapter. As far as classes go, it really doesn't matter what subjects you take, but I would say that, in general, the more you know about everything the better indexer you'd be.

Q. How has technology changed the field of indexing? How will the field change in the next decade or so?

A. In the early days of indexing, the index was created by using the good-old "index card," but those days are long gone. Today, indexes are created using dedicated indexing software that tremendously speeds the process and removes most of the tedious components of the process. Future developments will certainly be made in software, but the human element of creating an index will remain. Language has nuance and context that computers do not understand.

Intellectual Property Lawyers

OVERVIEW

Intellectual property lawyers focus on the protection of creative thought. Intellectual property (IP) lawyers may work with patents to protect their clients' inventions and discoveries; copyrights to protect works their clients have authored, such as text, music, or computer programs; and trademarks to protect brand names and symbols associated with their clients' businesses. IP attorneys may also work with companies to protect their trade secrets. IP lawyers are kept busy during periods of economic productivity, protecting emerging new ideas and creations such as Internet sites and scientific discoveries. According to the Franklin Pierce Law Center, the United States is the largest producer of intellectual property in the world.

HISTORY

Dating back to the 1700s, people have sought help to protect their ideas. Unfortunately, in the past both lawyers and clients were often frustrated in their attempts to gain support for patents and copyrights in court. The country as a whole, the court system, and Congress were intent on not allowing monopolies to gain control of innovative products or ideas. This fear of monopolization caused the patent holder to get little if any help or protection from the government. Within the past 20 years, however, Congress and judges have started to see innovative ideas and products as valuable for our trade status in the international market.

QUICK FACTS

School Subjects
English
Government
Speech

Personal Skills
Communication/ideas
Leadership/management

Work Environment
Primarily indoors
Primarily multiple locations

Minimum Education Level
Master's degree

Salary Range
$77,000 to $119,000 to
$200,000+

Certification or Licensing
Required by all states

Outlook
Faster than the average

DOT
110

GOE
04.02.01

NOC
4112

O*NET-SOC
23-1011.00

Attitudes are not the only things that have changed. Compared to the earliest years of inventions, innovative ideas, and patent seeking, huge amounts of intellectual property are now created and need protection daily. Intellectual property now includes music, computer software, written documents, programming code, and much more. Just as the volume and type of intellectual property has grown, so have the ways to steal it. Thieves today use home computers, digital equipment, and satellites. This boom in intellectual property and its need for protection have increased the demand for IP lawyers. Previously, IP law was a smaller segment of a law firm's business, so it was hired out to smaller boutique-type law firms. Now major firms and corporations have entire teams in-house to meet the demands of intellectual law.

The Internet has also been instrumental in creating a demand for these lawyers as they try to protect the use of online material.

THE JOB

Intellectual property lawyers have the task of protecting a client's creative interests, whether those interests are to patent a new product or to ensure that a copyright hasn't been infringed upon. IP lawyers may work in all areas of intellectual property law; however, many lawyers specialize in patent, trademark, copyright, or licensing law. Whichever area the IP attorney focuses on, some job duties are the same across the board. One of the IP lawyer's main tasks is to counsel clients. Usually this counseling concerns whether the intellectual property can be patented, trademarked, or copyrighted; the best method of protection for the individual property; and whether the product or idea being discussed will infringe on someone else's patent, trademark, or copyright. Another major task for an IP lawyer is the drafting of legal documents, such as patent applications and licensing agreements. Registered Patent Attorney Delbert Phillips states, "An IP lawyer drafts applications to the Patent Office and answers actions from the United States Patent Office by way of drafting amendments to the already filed application. Also, part of the job is drafting licenses and assignments (papers transferring ownership or giving permission for other people to practice the invention) for patent and trademarks."

The IP lawyer also serves clients by being their advocate before administrative bodies and courts. The IP lawyer's goal is to secure the rights of the client and then protect those rights if others violate them. Conversely, if the IP lawyer's client is accused of violating someone else's intellectual property rights, the IP lawyer defends the client.

IP lawyers may help their clients choose an Internet domain name or a trademark. They are often called upon to review advertising copy, press releases, and other official documents to ensure that there are no intellectual property problems.

IP lawyers work with a wide variety of clients, from an individual inventor or author to the CEO of a large publishing company. Those who work for corporations are usually in-house counsels concerned with decisions affecting the use of intellectual property within the company. IP lawyers working in universities assist scientists and researchers by identifying products and inventions that have potential in the marketplace.

If a client believes his or her rights to intellectual property have been infringed upon, the IP attorney must try to prove that someone else has taken or used the client's intellectual property without consent. On the other hand, if a client is accused of infringing on another's intellectual property rights, the lawyer must try to prove that the item in question didn't deserve a copyright, patent, or trademark in the first place or that the protection is invalid. Although lawsuits are commonplace today, most IP lawyers consider litigation the last step and try to settle differences outside the courtroom.

REQUIREMENTS

High School

Because intellectual property often deals with creations in the literary, scientific, engineering, and music worlds, a background in any of those areas will be helpful. If you are interested in combining a certain area with practicing law, you should focus on that area while in high school. "Take as many science courses as possible along with technical writing," recommends Delbert Phillips. "An IP lawyer must know basic scientific principles in order to draft the patent applications. It also helps if the student can become meticulous in thinking and in keeping track of records." Take courses in business, accounting, English, computers, and government as well.

Postsecondary Training

As in other areas of law, IP lawyers most often complete an undergraduate degree and then graduate from law school. For most types of intellectual property law, the undergraduate degree does not have to have a special focus. The exception to that is patent law. If you want to become a patent lawyer, you should major in science, engineering, or physics. Other technology-related courses will also be helpful.

To apply for almost any law school, you must first pass the Law School Admission Test (LSAT). The LSAT is an aptitude test used to predict how successful an individual will be in law school. Most law schools teach courses in intellectual property law, but some have IP sections and degrees, such as Columbia University School of Law, Franklin Pierce Law Center, and George Mason University Law School.

Certification or Licensing

After graduating from law school, you will be eligible to take the bar exam in any state. After passing the bar, you will be sworn in as an attorney and will then be eligible to practice law. Patent attorneys who practice patent law before the United States Patent Office must go a step further and obtain additional certification. Would-be patent lawyers must pass the patent bar exam. According to the American Bar Association, you must hold a bachelor's degree in engineering, physics, or the natural sciences (such as chemistry and biochemistry, hold a bachelor's degree in another subject, or have passed the Engineer in Training (EIT) test in order to be eligible to take the patent bar exam.

Other Requirements

IP lawyers should have excellent written and oral communication skills. In fact, the American Bar Foundation says a recent survey shows that law firms are more interested in these skills than the overall legal knowledge of the interviewee. Also, having command of foreign languages is crucial because IP lawyers work with products and ideas in international markets.

Phillips says that a patent lawyer who practices solo must be "a generalist who can understand mechanical engineering, basic electrical engineering, and rudimentary chemistry in order to draft the application and argue the merits during the amendment phase of intellectual law."

EXPLORING

IP law is a perfect career for someone who is interested in both science and technology and legal areas. Because of this duality, you can explore the career by focusing on the law side or on the science/technology side. To get experience on the law side, seek summer jobs and internships with law offices where you live. You may be able to get a part-time job as a legal assistant. Also check out your local business college for special prelaw programs that offer introductory law courses to the public. If you can't get any hands-on experience right away, ask your guidance counselor for help in setting up a tour of a local law office or arranging for an interview with a law professional. Any experience you can get writing technical or legal documents can also help, so don't rule out temporary jobs in any kind of business office.

If you have another interest that you hope to combine with law, try to get some hands-on experience in that area as well. If you are interested in science, for instance, join the science club at your school. Ask your science teacher about planning a field trip to anywhere you can learn about engineering. Take initiative and start an inventors club with your classmates to come up with new ideas and products.

EMPLOYERS

Intellectual property lawyers are in high demand with many types of employers. You'll find IP lawyers in major corporations (including publishing and media companies), law firms, universities, and government agencies. IP lawyers may also own their own businesses. The main employer of IP attorneys, however, is the United States Patent and Trademark Office (USPTO), which is part of the Department of Commerce. The USPTO employs lawyers as trademark examiners, patent examiners, and more. Other departments in the government that employ IP lawyers include the Departments of Defense, Interior, Justice, and Energy. IP lawyers can also find employment in the United States Copyright Office.

Although IP lawyers are in high demand all over the country, most work in large cities where the major corporations are headquartered. Other hot spots for IP lawyers include Washington, D.C., because of the government agencies located there, and Silicon Valley, California, because of its concentration of computer-related industry.

STARTING OUT

As in any area of law, internships and clerkships are usually the path to a quality job. For those interested in patent law specifically, applying for a clerkship in the United States Court of Appeals for the Federal Court in Washington, D.C., is a great way to gain experience. To apply for an unpaid, part-time internship during law school or soon after graduation, you should write directly to the court about six months in advance. To gain a full-time, paid clerkship position, law students should inquire sometime before the end of their second year. You can also apply for clerkships and internships with law firms. Another way to break into the IP law field is to get a job at the USPTO. Working directly with patents will put you in a better position for an IP job later in your career.

ADVANCEMENT

Most IP lawyers start out with internships and clerkships at firms or courts. In law firms, IP lawyers start out as low-rung associates and then advance as their experience and track records allow. Associates with successful reputations and many years of experience can become partners in the law firm. IP lawyers who work for universities may advance from assisting scientific and engineering groups to becoming professors of IP law. Whether in corporations, government agencies, or law firms, most IP lawyers, like other types of lawyers, are given more high profile cases and more important clients as they become more experienced.

EARNINGS

According to the American Intellectual Property Law Association, the average salary for an IP attorney in corporate offices and patent firms is $119,000 per year. Inexperienced IP lawyers can expect to make between $80,000 and $85,000, and those with the most experience and success will earn more than $180,000 per year. The median income for partners in private law firms is over $200,000 per year, while associates' salary is about $77,000. IP lawyers who own their own practices usually make $100,000 per year while salaries for those who work in law firms and corporations averaged slightly higher.

Almost all corporations, firms, and government agencies provide medical insurance, vacation, sick days, and holidays. Partners in large firms can expect other perks as well, including company cars, spending allowances, bonuses, and more depending on the firm.

WORK ENVIRONMENT

IP attorneys, like lawyers in other areas, have heavy workloads and work long hours. IP lawyers may spend hours poring over documents with few breaks. Many law firms have weekly goals for their lawyers that include the number of hours billed to the client. Some of these goals can be extremely demanding. Most of the lawyer's time is spent indoors meeting with clients, researching, or arguing in court. Depending on their position in the company or firm, IP lawyers may lead a team of lawyers or supervise a group of paralegals and associates.

OUTLOOK

The outlook for intellectual property law is promising. This field is relatively new and the demand for IP professionals doesn't show signs of slowing. The growth of the computer industry and the Internet have provided a great amount of work for IP lawyers. As new computer software and online media enters the market, IP lawyers will be needed to protect it. According to the American Bar Association, even if other markets that use the services of lawyers are softened by recession, the demand for IP lawyers will remain high. Because there will always be a need to protect the creative resources of the people, there will also be a need for IP lawyers.

FOR MORE INFORMATION

For information on all areas of law, law schools, the bar exam, and career guidance, contact
American Bar Association
321 North Clark Street
Chicago, IL 60610-4714
Tel: 800-285-2221
Email: askaba@abanet.org
http://www.abanet.org

To read the publications What Is a Patent, a Trademark and a Copyright? *and* Careers in IP Law, *visit the AIPLA's Web site.*
American Intellectual Property Law Association (AIPLA)
241 18th Street South, Suite 700
Arlington, VA 22202-3419
Tel: 703-415-0780
Email: aipla@aipla.org
http://www.aipla.org

For information about IP law and degree programs, contact
Franklin Pierce Law Center
Two White Street
Concord, NH 03301-4176
Tel: 603-228-1541
Email: admissions@piercelaw.edu
http://www.fplc.edu

For information on patent law, contact
National Association of Patent Practitioners
4680-18-i Monticello Avenue

PMB 101
Williamsburg, VA 23188-8214
Tel: 800-216-9588
http://www.napp.org

For information about IP, job opportunities, and recent press releases, contact the USPTO. Its Web site offers a link designed specifically for creative students interested in invention and includes contest information.
United States Patent and Trademark Office (USPTO)
PO Box 1450
Alexandria, VA 22313-1450
Tel: 800-786-9199
Email: usptoinfo@uspto.gov
http://www.uspto.gov

Lexicographers

OVERVIEW

Lexicographers research word usage and history, record citations, and write and edit entries for dictionaries. They are employed by major dictionary publishers and publishers of specialized dictionaries, such as medical, law, and foreign language dictionaries.

HISTORY

The earliest dictionaries were glossaries of Latin words with definitions in Old English, which was spoken before A.D. 1100. It wasn't until 1600 that monolingual dictionaries (lists of English words with English definitions) appeared and they included only difficult words. In the 18th century dictionaries began to include common words and their meanings, and also included pronunciations, etymologies, and parts of speech. Dictionaries continued to grow to cover the entire English vocabulary, and lexicographers amassed large collections of examples of word usage. Two of the most well-known lexicographers were Samuel Johnson, who published his *Dictionary* in 1755 and Noah Webster, whose greatest dictionary was published in 1828. During the 20th century, dictionaries added slang, technical, and regional language. Publishers developed different types of dictionaries for specific purposes and groups, such as pocket dictionaries and medical dictionaries.

Today, computers have made the work of lexicographers much easier. In research, they have access to huge databases—called corpora—of English words, rare words, example sentences, and grammatical information. In production, dictionaries are now stored in electronic databases, which can be easily updated and changed.

Experts predict that by 2050 all dictionaries will be in electronic form, eliminating space considerations and allowing for the inclusion of much more information, illustrations, and perhaps audio and video features. The basic idea of a dictionary, however, is not likely to change.

THE JOB

Lexicographers spend most of their time in research. They have to decide which words to include in a dictionary and what they mean. That decision is based on how often a word is used and how it is used. Lexicographers read newspapers, books, magazines, electronic publications, and a variety of other published materials, looking for new words, new meanings of existing words, spelling variations, and anything else that might help them decide whether a word belongs in a dictionary.

They mark words and the accompanying text that might explain how they are used and what they mean. The marked items are entered into a computer database and also recorded on cards or slips of paper, called citations. Each citation contains the word, an example of the word used in context, and bibliographic information about the source where the word and example were found.

During a dictionary editing process, lexicographers have to decide which existing entries can remain unchanged, which ones need revision, which entries to drop, and which new ones to add. All these decisions are based on information in the citations. A new word makes it into a dictionary only if there are enough citations to show that it is widely used. The citations must be from a wide variety of sources over a period of time. (Unlike other dictionaries, which contain words in current usage, the *Oxford English Dictionary* never drops an entry, but only revises and adds new words.)

REQUIREMENTS

High School

To prepare for a career as a lexicographer, take English, literature, and composition classes in high school. You should also familiarize yourself with word processing programs, either by taking a computer science class or by completing school assignments. History and foreign language classes will also help prepare you for this career.

Postsecondary Training

Lexicographers usually have at least a bachelor's degree in linguistics, English, foreign languages, or history. Some, however, have advanced degrees in other subjects, and this education gives them the expertise to work on scientific entries, for example, or on a dictionary specifically for the chemical industry.

Other Requirements

Lexicographers need to be detail-oriented, persistent, and precise in research and writing. They could accurately be described as word detectives.

EXPLORING

To learn more about this profession, you should visit libraries to read dictionaries of all kinds, as well as other types of publications. Try to expand your vocabulary by adding at least one new word a day. Take advantage of any clubs or extracurricular activities that will give you a chance to write or edit. Joining the school newspaper staff is a great way to explore different tasks in publishing. You might also ask your English teacher or guidance counselor to set up an information interview with a lexicographer.

EMPLOYERS

There are many lexicographers who work full time for the major dictionary publishers, such as Merriam Webster Inc. (*Merriam Webster's Collegiate Dictionary*), Oxford University Press (*Oxford English Dictionary*), and Houghton Mifflin (*American Heritage Dictionary of the English Language*). Others work for publishers of the numerous specialized dictionaries, such as medical, law, and foreign language dictionaries. There are also many lexicographers who work on a freelance basis. Small publishers and organizations often hire freelance lexicographers to compile a dictionary on a particular subject, but even the major dictionary publishers hire a number of freelancers on an ongoing basis to research new words and new meanings for old words.

STARTING OUT

New lexicographers often start out at dictionary publishers as junior members of a lexicographic team. Others may enter the publishing industry as editorial assistants, proofreaders, and editors and gradually move into this career. Freelance lexicographers begin by soliciting work from dictionary publishers. To gain experience and build client relationships, they usually have to accept small jobs at relatively low pay rates.

Books to Read

Bejoint, Henri. *Modern Lexicography: An Introduction.* New York: Oxford University Press, 2000.

Jackson, Howard. *Lexicography: An Introduction.* New York: Routledge, 2002.

Landau, Sidney I. *Dictionaries: The Art and Craft of Lexicography.* 2d ed. New York: Cambridge University Press, 2004.

Mugglestone, Lynda (ed.) *Lexicography and the OED: Pioneers in the Untrodden Forest.* New York: Oxford University Press, 2002.

Murray, K. M. Elisabeth, and Burchfield, R. W. *Caught in the Web of Words: James Murray and the Oxford English Dictionary.* New Haven, Conn.: Yale University Press, 2001.

ADVANCEMENT

As they gain experience, junior lexicographers at dictionary publishers can eventually advance to positions of higher responsibility. They might eventually supervise a team of lexicographers or manage an editorial department. Other lexicographers might make lateral career moves to the position of editor or writer. Experienced freelance lexicographers may charge higher rates or take on more prestigious assignments as their level of expertise increases.

EARNINGS

The earnings of lexicographers are comparable to other writers and editors. According to the U.S. Department of Labor, mean annual earnings for salaried writers and authors were $46,420 in 2005, and median annual earnings for salaried editors were $45,510. Salaries ranged from less than $24,320 to more than $89,940.

WORK ENVIRONMENT

Lexicographers work in office settings or at home. They spend most of their time reading books, magazines, and other materials and working on their computers. Lexicographers employed by dictionary publishers usually work a standard 40-hour week. Freelance lexicographers have more flexible hours. They might work 12 hours one day, and only four the next day. Lexicographers may have to work extra hours to complete projects on deadline.

OUTLOOK

According to the *Career Guide to Industries*, employment in the publishing industry is expected to grow by 7 percent through 2014, which is lower than the 14 percent growth that is predicted for all industries. Despite this prediction, employment for experienced lexicographers should remain relatively stable over the next decade. Lexicographers are important players in the creation and revision of dictionaries, and although computers have made the work of lexicographers easier, there is little chance that technological advances will replace the need for these workers.

FOR MORE INFORMATION

This is an organization of lexicographers, writers, linguists, translators, librarians, and others interested in dictionaries. It publishes a semiannual newsletter, an annual journal, and a membership directory.

Dictionary Society of North America
University of Wisconsin-Madison
6129 H. C. White Hall
600 North Park Street
Madison, WI 53706-1403
Tel: 608-265-0532
http://polyglot.lss.wisc.edu/dsna

Literary Agents

OVERVIEW

Literary agents serve as intermediaries between writers and potential employers such as publishers and television producers. They also represent actors, artists, athletes, musicians, politicians, and other public figures who may seek to undertake writing endeavors. In essence, agents sell a product: their clients' creative talent. In addition to finding work for their clients, agents also may negotiate contracts, pursue publicity, and advise clients in their careers. The majority of literary agents work in New York and Los Angeles, and many others work in San Francisco, Chicago, and Miami. There are approximately 21,000 agents and business managers of artists, performers, and athletes in the United States. Literary agents make up a small percentage of this group.

HISTORY

The business of promoting writers is a product of the 20th century. Modern mass publishing and distribution systems, as well as the advent of the radio, television, and motion picture industries, have created a market for the writer's art that did not exist before. In the past, movie studios used staff writers. Today, independent writers create novels, magazine articles, screenplays, and scripts. It was perhaps only appropriate that brokers should emerge to bring together people who need each other: creators and producers. These brokers are literary agents.

THE JOB

Most agents can be divided into two broad groups: those who represent clients on a case-by-case basis and those who have intensive,

QUICK FACTS

School Subjects
Business
English

Personal Skills
Artistic
Communication/ideas
Leadership/management

Work Environment
Primarily indoors
One location with some
    travel

Minimum Education Level
High school diploma

Salary Range
$20,000 to $53,800 to
    $87,630+

Certification or Licensing
None available

Outlook
About as fast as the average

DOT
191

GOE
01.01.01

NOC
6411

O*NET-SOC
13-1011.00

ongoing partnerships with clients. Literary agents typically do not have long-term relationships with clients except for established authors. They may work with writers just one time, electing to represent them only after reading manuscripts and determining their viability. Literary agents market their clients' manuscripts to editors, publishers, and television and movie producers, among other buyers. Many of the most prestigious magazines and newspapers will not consider material unless an agent submits it. Busy editors rely on agents to screen manuscripts so that only the best, most professional product reaches them. Sometimes editors go directly to agents with editorial assignments, knowing that the agents will be able to find the best writer for the job.

After taking on a project, such as a book proposal, play, magazine article, or screenplay, agents approach publishers and producers in writing, by phone, or in person and try to convince these decision-makers to use their clients' work. When a publisher or other producer accepts a proposal, agents may negotiate contracts and rights, such as translation and excerpt rights, on behalf of their clients. Rather than pay authors directly, publishers pay their agents, who deduct their commission (anywhere from 4 to 20 percent of the total amount) and return the rest to the author.

Agents who represent established writers perform additional duties for their clients, such as directing them to useful resources, evaluating drafts and offering guidance, speaking for them in matters that must be decided in their absence, and in some instances serving as arbiters between coauthors. Also, to ensure that writers devote as much time as possible to their creative work, agents take care of such business as bookkeeping, processing income checks, and preparing tax forms.

REQUIREMENTS

High School

In order to identify and represent the best writers, you need to be well-versed in classic and modern literature and have strong writing skills yourself. While in high school, take classes in literature and composition. Theater and music classes are also beneficial if you are interested in screenplays and scripts. Business, accounting, and mathematics classes will help you develop skills that will help you to operate your business and the financial affairs of your clients.

Postsecondary Training

Desirable areas of study in college include liberal arts, performing arts, and business administration. It is also helpful to study law, although agents need not be lawyers. A college degree is not necessary, but would-be agents with a degree are more likely to be hired than those without a college education.

Other Requirements

Agents need not have any specific education or technical skills, but you must have a knack for recognizing and promoting marketable talent. You must be familiar with the needs of publishers so as to approach them with the most appropriate and timely manuscript. You must be persistent without crossing over the line to harassment, for you must not alienate any of the publishers you will want to contact in the future.

Because continued success depends on the ability to maintain good relationships with clients and potential employers for their clients, you must have good people skills; you must be able to interact tactfully and amicably with a wide variety of people, from demanding clients to busy editors. Moreover, because artists' careers have their ups and downs and production and publishing are fields with high turnover rates, you should not become complacent. You must be flexible, adaptive, and able to establish new relationships quickly and with finesse.

EXPLORING

If you are interested in literary management you can acquaint yourself with current trends in book publishing and with the kinds of books that particular publishing houses issue by working part time at bookstores and libraries. If you live in a big city, you may be able to get a job with a book or magazine publisher. Some literary agents also sponsor internships.

EMPLOYERS

Approximately 21,000 agents are employed in the United States. Literary agents make up a small percentage of this group. Literary agents work for established large or small agencies, although many are self-employed. Los Angeles and New York are the country's leading entertainment centers, and most agents work in either of those two cities. Some agencies have branch offices in other large U.S. cities and affiliate offices overseas, especially in London.

STARTING OUT

Employment within a production facility, publishing house, or entertainment center is a good beginning for agents because it provides an insider's knowledge of agents' target markets. The other optimum approach is to send resumes to any and all agencies and to be willing to start at the bottom, probably as an office worker, then working up to the position of subagent, in order to learn the field.

ADVANCEMENT

How far agents advance depends almost entirely on their entrepreneurial skills. Ability alone isn't enough; successful agents must be persistent and ambitious. In addition to proving themselves to their agency superiors and clients, they must earn the trust and respect of decision makers in the marketplace, such as publishers and producers. Once agents earn the confidence of a number of successful writers, they can strike out on their own and perhaps even establish their own agencies.

EARNINGS

Literary agents generally earned between $20,000 and $60,000 annually, with a rare few making hundreds of thousands of dollars a year. Because independent agents take a percentage of their clients' earnings (4 to 20 percent), their livelihoods are contingent upon the success of their clients, which is in turn contingent on the agents' ability to promote talent. Some beginning agents can go as long as a year without making any money at all, but, if at the end of that time, their clients begin to gain notice, the agents' investment of time may well pay off.

The U.S. Department of Labor reports that agents and business managers of artists, performers, and athletes earned a median salary of $53,800 a year in 2005. The highest paid 25 percent earned $87,630 or more, while the lowest paid 10 percent earned $25,840 or less.

According to the Association of Authors' Representatives, New York agency assistants typically earn beginning salaries of about $20,000. Sometimes agency staffers working on commission actually can earn more money than their bosses.

WORK ENVIRONMENT

Agents' hours are often uncertain, for in addition to fairly regular office hours, they often must meet on weekends and evenings with

Publishing Industry Employment

Industry Segment	Employment
Newspapers	55.8 percent
Periodicals	21.0 percent
Book publishing	11.9 percent
Directory and mailing lists	7.0 percent
Other publishers	4.3 percent

Source: U.S. Department of Labor, 2004

clients and editors with whom they are trying to build relationships. The majority of their time, however, is spent in the office on the phone. Novices can expect no more than a cubicle, while established agents may enjoy luxurious office suites.

Established agents may frequently travel internationally to meet with clients, to scout out new talent, and find new opportunities for their talent.

OUTLOOK

Agents work in an extremely competitive field. Most agents who attempt to go into business for themselves fail within one year. Most job openings within agencies are the result of turnover, rather than the development of new positions. There are many candidates for few positions.

FOR MORE INFORMATION

For information on the duties, responsibilities, and ethical expectations of agents, and for AAR's newsletter, contact or visit the following Web site

Association of Authors' Representatives Inc. (AAR)
676A Ninth Avenue, #312
New York, NY 10036-3602
Tel: 212-840-5777
Email: aarinc@mindspring.com
http://www.aar-online.org

To read answers to frequently asked questions about agents and publishing, visit the following Web site

Adler & Robin Books
http://www.adlerbooks.com/mostask.html

To access the latest news on book publishing, marketing, and selling, visit the Publishers Weekly *Web site.*

Publishers Weekly
http://www.publishersweekly.com

Online Producers

OVERVIEW

Online producers are responsible for organizing and presenting information that is available on Web sites. They edit and/or write news stories, arrange the text, and any accompanying photos for online publication. They sometimes work with other workers to incorporate slideshows, background music, or audio interviews to better complement a story. While many online producers are employed in journalism, a growing number of producers find work managing corporate Web sites for advertising agencies, employment firms, pharmaceutical companies, nonprofits, and other organizations. Online producers are also referred to as *content producers* and *online editors*.

HISTORY

The manner in which people receive news and other information has changed with the popularity of computers and access to the Internet. People crave news—from breaking stories to real-time baseball scores—and are no longer willing to wait until the next morning's edition of their favorite newspaper to stay up to speed with the world around them. Also, portable computers and PDAs made access to the Internet possible while commuting to and from work. Web-based editions of newspapers, television stations, magazines, and radio stations have quickly found an audience. Online producers, professionals with writing and editing skills, as well as computer savvy, are needed to maintain these sites with well written and presented articles. Additionally, online producers are in demand in non-journalistic settings as many businesses and other organizations seek a place on the Internet.

THE JOB

Online producers working in journalism are responsible for the daily writing/editing and presentation of information appearing on their organization's Web sites. Most forms of media—newspapers, magazines, television, and radio—have a Web-based equivalent where people can access news and information on a 24-hour basis. Online producers take news articles originally published in that day's paper or broadcast, and translate them into appropriate content for the organization's Web site. If new developments have occurred since the story was first printed, they are incorporated into the online version. Special coding is added to the article, most often HTML, which allows the text to be posted on a Web site. Links or related keywords are added so the article will show up in searches and archives.

The Web version of a story must be presented in a different way than it is on paper—text is often edited to be more concise and engaging to the reader. The layout of the entire article is key—if it doesn't grab the reader's attention, the story may be ignored by online readers. Online producers may choose to include features such as photos, video, animation, music, or art. Since space is not an issue on the Web, many articles run with sidebars, photos, and other features not originally included in the print or broadcast edition. Online producers often work with multimedia producers to create special content packages such as videos or an audio slide show—a series of photos presented with an audio voiceover—to further enhance a story. Other stories lend themselves to special art provided by different vendors. Online producers, working with the advertising and technical departments, decide on which pieces to purchase and use. Sports sections, for example, oftentimes use team rosters and statistics to complement special event coverage such as the Super Bowl, the World Series, or the Olympic Games.

On an average shift, online producers can expect to produce about two to four dozen stories. Many of the stories are filtered from the day's print edition, but some will be reported directly from the field, or from newswire services. Some online producers, especially at smaller companies, are responsible for producing all news stories, regardless of subject. Online producers employed at large media companies may be assigned a specific beat or area of expertise such as world news or sports. Teamwork is part of the job as well. When an important story unfolds or a special edition is being created to cover a major event—such as the death of a religious leader or a presidential election—online producers will work with other members of the editorial staff to get the news posted as quickly as possible.

Online producers also work in the corporate world at companies that range from advertising agencies to national retail chains. Producers employed in this capacity deal more with the design and maintenance of the Web site, or in some cases, multiple sites. An online producer working on a retail Web site coordinates with the company's creative merchandising team to launch a new product line, or shopping portal. They monitor the site to make sure links are working properly, and troubleshoot any problems. Online producers working for a school or professional organization may be responsible for setting up and moderating forums and chat rooms as well as creating online banners, online company newsletters, and posting relevant news articles regarding their employer.

REQUIREMENTS

High School

Solid computer skills will give you the edge over other candidates. Prepare yourself by enrolling in every computer class your school has to offer, from programming to Web site design. Familiarize yourself with different software programs such as Adobe Photoshop, Macromedia DreamWeaver, or Macromedia HomeSite and different markup languages such as HTML. Round out your education with classes such as business, math, and English. Since many online producers have a journalism background, you'll need strong reporting, writing, and editing skills to keep up with the competition. Any classes that require written reports as regular assignments are wise choices.

Postsecondary Training

While there are many routes of study in preparation for this career, many online producers enter the field after earning a bachelor's degree in journalism. In fact, many schools now offer Web-based media classes as an elective to their traditional journalism studies. Northwestern University's Medill School of Journalism, for example, now offers a New Media concentration alongside traditional print, broadcast, and magazine journalism curricula at the undergraduate and graduate level. Besides the demands of good reporting and writing, New Media students are taught various computer languages, publishing software, and interactive tools needed to present news online, as well as how to address the challenges of instant, space unlimited publishing. Check out Medill's Web site (http://www.medill.northwestern.edu/journalism/newmedia/index.html) for more information.

Other Requirements

Do you perform well under pressure? Can you quickly change gears and focus on a completely different project without complaining or losing momentum? Are you self-motivated and an independent worker, yet capable of being a team player? If you answer yes to these questions, you have some of the skills that are necessary for success in this industry.

EXPLORING

Creating your own Web site is an excellent way to explore this career. Not only will you gain experience in Web design, coding, and different software programs, you'll have total editorial control.

Does your school paper have a Web site? If not, take the initiative and build one. As online producer for this project, you can add photo slideshows of the school prom, add a team roster graphic for the winning basketball team, and spice up your site with links to school clubs and organizations.

You should also surf the Web to view existing news and corporate Web sites. Write down what you like and dislike about each. Are the links relevant? Is the story portrayed in a concise, yet informative manner? If given the chance, what improvements would you make?

You might also consider becoming a student member of the Online News Association, a professional organization for online journalism professionals. Besides presenting the latest industry news, the association's Web site offers a wealth of information on available internships, school programs, conferences, and forums. Log onto http://journalist.org/about/archives/000128.php for more information regarding a membership at the student level.

STARTING OUT

A job as an assistant or associate online producer is a common starting point for this career. Many companies hiring online producers require at least three years experience in Web journalism. Internships are your best bet to gain experience and training as well as valuable industry contacts for the future.

Check with your school's career counselor for possible leads on summer internships; some publications or companies may hire high school students. Even if you spend your working day running for coffee or answering phones, at least you'll be in the company of industry professionals. Contact your local newspaper to see if any part-time employment opportunities are available during the school year or summer vacation.

Also, check with associations for job leads. The Online News Association posts job openings nationwide. Poynter Online (http://www.poynter.org/default.asp), besides being a great resource of industry news, offers seminars, fellowships, tip sheets, and links to employment possibilities.

ADVANCEMENT

Larger publications promote experienced online producers to senior or executive status. Those employed at regional publications could seek jobs at larger publications with broader news coverage. Online producers working in the corporate realm could advance their careers by working for larger, more diverse companies, or those with multiple Web sites.

EARNINGS

Although no specific salary statistics are available for online producers, earnings for these professionals are generally similar to that of traditional editors—although online editors may earn slightly more than their print counterparts. According to the U.S. Department of Labor, the median yearly income of traditional editors was $45,510 in 2005. The lowest 10 percent of all editors earned less than $26,910; the highest 10 percent earned more than $85,230. Online producers typically receive benefits such as vacation and sick days and health insurance.

WORK ENVIRONMENT

Online producers—especially those in journalism—work in hectic, fast paced environments. Deadlines are short and may come at any time of the day or night. Online producers must be able to drop a current project, shift gears, and quickly focus on a breaking story. Most online producers have more editorial control as opposed to editors on the print side of a publication. Since much of their work is done after editorial offices have closed for the day, they oftentimes make key decisions on what stories are posted at the organization's Web site.

Web sites operate 24-hours a day, seven days a week. News is often posted minutes after it has occurred. Work shifts are scheduled to accommodate this, and may vary from week to week. Nontraditional work hours can be physically exhausting and, at times, affect an online producer's personal life.

OUTLOOK

The Web has already had a major impact on how people receive and access their news and information. And with the popularity of portable computers and cell phones, and PDAs with Internet access, the number of people turning to Web-based news and information is expected to grow. Most, if not all, forms of traditional media—newspapers, magazines, and television—have a Web-based counterpart. And with more corporate, small business, and professional organizations seeking a presence on the Web, the need for capable online producers is certain to increase.

Industry experts predict that some duties of online producers, such as story production and layout, may be eventually automated, leaving producers more time for original reporting in the field. Also, look for online producers to enjoy increasing opportunities with startup online publications that do not have ties to a print or broadcast entity.

FOR MORE INFORMATION

For information on its New Media program, contact
Medill School of Journalism
Northwestern University
1845 Sheridan Road
Evanston, IL 60208-2101
Tel: 847-467-1882
Email: medill-admis@northwestern.edu
http://www.medill.northwestern.edu/journalism/newmedia/
    index.html

For information on internships, school programs, and memberships, contact
Online News Association
PO Box 2002, Radio City Station
New York, NY 10101-2022
Tel: 646-290-7900
http://www.onlinenewsassociation.org

For information on fellowships, seminars, and employment opportunities, visit
Poynter Online
http://www.poynter.org/default.asp

Photo Editors

OVERVIEW

Photo editors are responsible for the look of final photographs to be published in a book or periodical or that are posted on the Internet. They make photo assignments, judge and alter pictures to meet assignment needs, and make sure all deadlines are met. They work for publishers, advertising agencies, photo stock agencies, greeting card companies, and any employer that relies heavily on visual images to sell its products or services.

HISTORY

For as long as photos have been in print, photo editors have been needed to evaluate them and delegate shooting assignments. In the early days of photography (the late 1800s), the jobs of photographer and editor were generally combined. On the staffs of early newspapers, it was not uncommon to have a story editor evaluate and place photos, or for a reporter to shoot his or her own accompanying photos as well as edit them for print. However, the need for a separate photo editor has become apparent as visual elements have become a larger part of print and online publications, advertisements, and even political campaigns. The trained eye and technical know-how of a photo editor is now an essential part of newsroom staffs and corporate offices everywhere.

QUICK FACTS

School Subjects
Art
Computer science

Personal Skills
Artistic
Communication/ideas

Work Environment
Primarily indoors
Primarily one location

Minimum Education Level
Some postsecondary training

Salary Range
$43,048 to $58,240 to $74,721+

Certification or licensing
None available

Outlook
About as fast as the average

DOT
143

GOE
01.02.03

NOC
5221

O*NET-SOC
27-4021.00, 27-4021.01, 27-4021.02

THE JOB

The final look of a print or online publication is the result of many workers. The photo editor is responsible for the pictures you see in these publications. They work with photographers, reporters, authors, copy editors, and company executives to make sure final photos help to illustrate, enlighten, or inspire the reader.

Photo editors, though knowledgeable in photography, generally leave the shooting to staff or contract photographers. Editors meet with their managers or clients to determine the needs of the project and brainstorm ideas for photos that will meet the project's goals. After picture ideas have been discussed, editors give photographers assignments, always including a firm deadline for completion. Most editors work for companies that face firm deadlines; if the editor doesn't have pictures to work with in time, the whole project is held up.

Once photos have arrived, the editor gets to work, using computer software to crop or enlarge shots, alter the coloring of images, or emphasize the photographer's use of shadows or light. All this work requires knowledge of photography, an aesthetic eye, and an awareness of the project's needs. Editors working for a newspaper must be sure to print photos that are true to life, while editors working for a fine-arts publication can alter images to create a more abstract effect.

Photo editors also use photo stock agencies to meet project needs. Depending on the size and type of company the editor works for, he or she might not have a staff of photographers to work with. Stock agencies fill this need. Editors can browse stock photos for sale online or in brochures. Even with purchased photos, the editor still has to make sure the image fits the needs and space of the project.

In addition to working with photos, editors take on managerial tasks, such as assigning deadlines, organizing the office, ordering supplies, training employees, and overseeing the work of others. Along with copy and project editors, the photo editor is in contact with members of upper management or outside clients, and thus he or she is responsible for communicating their needs and desires to other workers.

REQUIREMENTS

High School

In addition to photography classes, take illustration and other art classes to develop an artistic eye and familiarize yourself with other forms of visual aids that are used in publications. Math classes will come in handy, as editors have to exactly measure the size and resolution of photos. To be able to determine what photo will meet the needs of a project, you will have to do a lot of reading, so English and communications classes are useful. Last but certainly not least, computer science classes will be invaluable. As an editor, you will work with computers almost daily and must be comfortable with art, layout, and word processing programs.

Postsecondary Training

While not required, most large and prestigious companies will want editors with a college degree in photography, visual art, or computer science. Employers will also want experience, so be sure to get as much exposure working on a publication as possible while in school. Other options are to go to a community college for a degree program; many offer programs in art or computer science that should be sufficient.

You should also be more than familiar with photo editing software such as Adobe PhotoShop, Apple iPhoto, and Corel Photo-Paint, just to name a few.

Other Requirements

In addition to technical know-how, you should also be adept at working with people and for people. As an editor, you will often be the liaison between the client or upper management and the reporters and photographers working for you. You need to be able to communicate the needs of the project to all those working on it.

EXPLORING

To see if this career might be for you, explore your interests. Get involved with your school yearbook or newspaper. Both of these publications often appoint student photo editors to assist with photo acquisitions and layout. You should also try your hand at photography. To be a knowledgeable and successful editor, you need to know the medium in which you work.

You could also try to speak to a professional photo editor about his or her work. Ask a teacher or your counselor to set up a meeting, and think of questions to ask the editor ahead of time.

EMPLOYERS

Photo editors work for any organization that produces publications or online newsletters or has a Web site with many photos. This includes publishing houses, large corporations, Web site developers, nonprofit organizations, and the government. A large percentage of photo editors also work for stock photo agencies, either as staff photographers or as freelancers.

STARTING OUT

Photo editors often start out as photographers, staff writers, or other lower-level editors. They have to gain experience in their area of work, whether it is magazine publishing or Web site development, to be able to choose the right photos for their projects.

ADVANCEMENT

Photo editors advance by taking on more supervisory responsibility for their department or by working on larger projects for high-end clients. These positions generally command more money and can lead to chief editorial jobs. Freelance editors advance by working for more clients and charging more money for their services.

EARNINGS

Earnings for photo editors will vary depending on where they work. Salary.com reports that in March 2007, the median expected salary for a typical photo editor was approximately $58,240, but it ranged from less than $43,048 to more than $74,721. If the editor is employed by a corporation, stock photo agency, or other business, he or she typically will be entitled to health insurance, vacation time, and other benefits. Self-employed editors have to provide their own health and life insurance, but they can make their own schedules.

WORK ENVIRONMENT

Editors typically work in a comfortable office setting, with computers and other tools nearby. Depending on the workplace, the environment can be quiet and slow, or busy with plenty of interruptions. Deadline pressures can make the job of photo editing hectic at times. Tight production schedules may leave editors with little time to acquire photos or contract work out to photographers. Editors may have a quick turn-around time from when completed photos land on their desk to when the publication has to be sent to the printer. However, unless the editor works for a daily paper or weekly magazine, these busy periods are generally accompanied by slower periods with looser schedules. A good photo editor is flexible and able to work under both conditions.

OUTLOOK

Photo editing has been a popular and in-demand field for many years. More and more companies are relying on Web presence,

Stock Photo Agencies on the Web

Comstock Images
http://www.comstock.com/web/default.asp

Corbis
http://pro.corbis.com

Creatas Images
http://www.creatas.com

Dynamic Graphics
http://www.dgusa.com

Getty Images
http://creative.gettyimages.com/source/home/home.aspx

Index Stock Imagery
http://www.indexstock.com

Landov
http://www.landov.com

RubberBall Productions
http://www.rubberball.com

SuperStock
http://www.superstock.com

Thinkstock
http://www.thinkstock.com/web/default.asp

complete with engaging visuals, to sell their products or services. Photo editors will also always be needed to help create a polished look to a printed publication, selecting just the right photos to deliver the right message to readers.

Though computers have revolutionized the way that photo editors work—bringing their work from paper to screen—they have also caused some problems. Improved software technology now makes it possible for virtually anyone to scan or download an image and alter it to any specifications. However, most professional publications will still hire photo editors with expertise and a trained eye to do this work.

FOR MORE INFORMATION

The NPPA maintains a job bank, provides educational information, and makes insurance available to its members. It also publishes News Photographer *magazine.*
National Press Photographers Association (NPPA)
3200 Croasdaile Drive, Suite 306
Durham, NC 27705-2588
Tel: 919-383-7246
Email: info@nppa.org
http://www.nppa.org

This organization provides training, publishes its own magazine, and offers various services for its members.
Professional Photographers of America
229 Peachtree Street, NE, Suite 2200
Atlanta, GA 30303-1608
Tel: 800-786-6277
Email: csc@ppa.com
http://www.ppa.com

This organization provides workshops, conferences, and other professional meetings for "management or leadership-level people responsible for overseeing photography at their publications." Visit its Web site to read articles on news and developments within the industry.
Associated Press Photo Managers
Email: appm@ap.org
http://www.apphotomanagers.org

Check out this site to see examples of high-quality stock photos.
Stock Solution's Top Photo Site of the Week
http://www.tssphoto.com/foto_week.html

Photographers

OVERVIEW

Photographers take and sometimes develop and print pictures of people, places, objects, and events, using a variety of cameras and photographic equipment. They work in the publishing, advertising, public relations, science, and business industries, as well as provide personal photographic services. They may also work as fine artists. There are approximately 129,000 photographers employed in the United States.

HISTORY

The word *photograph* means "to write with light." Although the art of photography goes back only about 150 years, the two Greek words that were chosen and combined to refer to this skill quite accurately describe what it does.

The discoveries that led eventually to photography began early in the 18th century when a German scientist, Dr. Johann H. Schultze, experimented with the action of light on certain chemicals. He found that when these chemicals were covered by dark paper they did not change color, but when they were exposed to sunlight, they darkened. A French painter named Louis Daguerre became the first photographer in 1839, using silver-iodide-coated plates and a small box. To develop images on the plates, Daguerre exposed them to mercury vapor. The daguerreotype, as these early photographs came to be known, took minutes to expose and the developing process was directly to the plate. There were no prints made.

Although the daguerreotype was the sensation of its day, it was not until George Eastman invented a simple camera and flexible roll film that photography began to come into widespread use in the

QUICK FACTS

School Subjects
Art
Chemistry

Personal Skills
Artistic
Communication/ideas

Work Environment
Indoors and outdoors
Primarily multiple locations

Minimum Education Level
Some postsecondary training

Salary Range
$15,240 to $37,230 to $53,900+

Certification or Licensing
None available

Outlook
About as fast as the average

DOT
143

GOE
01.02.03

NOC
5221

O*NET-SOC
27-4021.00, 27-4021.01, 27-4021.02

Photographers should have manual dexterity, good eyesight and color vision, and artistic ability. *(Jim Whitmer Photography)*

late 1800s. After exposing this film to light and developing it with chemicals, the film revealed a color-reversed image, which is called a negative. To make the negative positive (aka: print a picture), light must be shone though the negative onto light-sensitive paper. This process can be repeated to make multiple copies of an image from one negative.

One of the most important developments in recent years is digital photography. In digital photography, instead of using film, pictures are recorded on microchips, which can then be downloaded onto a computer's hard drive. They can be manipulated in size, color, and shape, virtually eliminating the need for a darkroom. In the professional world, digital images are primarily used in electronic publishing and advertising since printing technology hasn't quite caught up with camera technology. However, printing technology is also advancing and even amateur photographers can use digital cameras and home printers to shoot, manipulate, correct, and print snapshots.

THE JOB

Photography is both an artistic and technical occupation. There are many variables in the process that a knowledgeable photographer can manipulate to produce a clear image or a more abstract work of fine art. First, photographers know how to use cameras and can adjust focus, shutter speeds, aperture, lenses, and filters. They know about the types and speeds of films. Photographers also know about light and shadow, deciding when to use available natural light and when to set up artificial lighting to achieve desired effects.

Some photographers send their film to laboratories, but some develop their own negatives and make their own prints. These processes require knowledge about chemicals such as developers and fixers and how to use enlarging equipment. Photographers must also be familiar with the large variety of papers available for printing photographs, all of which deliver a different effect. Most photographers continually experiment with photographic processes to improve their technical proficiency or to create special effects.

Digital photography is a relatively new development. With this new technology, film is replaced by microchips that record pictures in digital format. Pictures can then be downloaded onto a computer's hard drive. Photographers use special software to manipulate the images on screen. Digital photography is used primarily for electronic publishing and advertising.

Photographers usually specialize in one of several areas: portraiture, commercial and advertising photography, photojournalism, fine art, educational photography, or scientific photography. There are subspecialties within each of these categories. A *scientific photographer*, for example, may specialize in aerial or underwater photography. A *commercial photographer* may specialize in food or fashion photography.

Some photographers write for trade and technical journals, teach photography in schools and colleges, act as representatives of photographic equipment manufacturers, sell photographic equipment and supplies, produce documentary films, or do freelance work.

REQUIREMENTS

High School

While in high school, take as many art classes and photography classes that are available. Chemistry is useful for understanding developing and printing processes. You can learn about photo manipulation software and digital photography in computer classes, and business classes will help if you are considering a freelance career.

Postsecondary Training

Formal educational requirements depend upon the nature of the photographer's specialty. For instance, photographic work in scientific and engineering research generally requires an engineering background with a degree from a recognized college or institute.

A college education is not required to become a photographer, although college training probably offers the most promising assurance of success in fields such as industrial, news, or scientific photography. There are degree programs at the associate's, bachelor's, and master's levels. Many schools offer courses in cinematography, although very few have programs leading to a degree in this specialty. Many men and women, however, become photographers with no formal education beyond high school.

To become a photographer, you should have a broad technical understanding of photography plus as much practical experience with cameras as possible. Take many different kinds of photographs with a variety of cameras and subjects. Learn how to develop photographs and, if possible, build your own darkroom or rent one. Experience in picture composition, cropping prints (cutting images to a desired size), enlarging, and retouching are all valuable.

Other Requirements
You should possess manual dexterity, good eyesight and color vision, and artistic ability to succeed in this line of work. You need an eye for form and line, an appreciation of light and shadow, and the ability to use imaginative and creative approaches to photographs or film, especially in commercial work. In addition, you should be patient and accurate and enjoy working with detail.

Self-employed (or freelance) photographers need good business skills. They must be able to manage their own studios, including hiring and managing assistants and other employees, keeping records, and maintaining photographic and business files. Marketing and sales skills are also important to a successful freelance photography business.

EXPLORING
Photography is a field that anyone with a camera can explore. To learn more about this career, you can join high school camera clubs, yearbook or newspaper staffs, photography contests, and community hobby groups. You can also seek a part-time or summer job in a camera shop or work as a developer in a laboratory or processing center.

EMPLOYERS
About 129,000 photographers work in the United States, more than half of whom are self-employed. Most jobs for photographers are

provided by photographic or commercial art studios; other employers include newspapers and magazines, radio and TV broadcasting, government agencies, and manufacturing firms. Colleges, universities, and other educational institutions employ photographers to prepare promotional and educational materials.

STARTING OUT

Some photographers enter the field as apprentices, trainees, or assistants. Trainees may work in a darkroom, camera shop, or developing laboratory. They may move lights and arrange backgrounds for a commercial or portrait photographer or motion picture photographer. Assistants spend many months learning this kind of work before they move into a job behind a camera.

Many large cities offer schools of photography, which may be a good way to start in the field. Beginning press photographers may work for one of the many newspapers and magazines published in their area. Other photographers choose to go into business for themselves as soon as they have finished their formal education. Setting up a studio may not require a large capital outlay, but beginners may find that success does not come easily.

ADVANCEMENT

Because photography is such a diversified field, there is no usual way in which to get ahead. Those who begin by working for someone else may advance to owning their own businesses. Commercial photographers may gain prestige as more of their pictures are placed in well-known trade journals or popular magazines. Press photographers may advance in salary and the kinds of important news stories assigned to them. A few photographers may become celebrities in their own right by making contributions to the art world or the sciences.

EARNINGS

The U.S. Department of Labor reports that salaried photographers employed in newspaper, book, and directory publishing earned mean annual salaries of $37,230 in 2005. Salaries for all photographers ranged from less than $15,240 to more than $53,900.

Self-employed photographers often earn more than salaried photographers, but their earnings depend on general business conditions. In addition, self-employed photographers do not receive the benefits that a company provides its employees.

Scientific photographers, who combine training in science with photographic expertise, usually start at higher salaries than other photographers. They also usually receive consistently larger advances in salary than do others, so that their income, both as beginners and as experienced photographers, place them well above the average in their field. Photographers in salaried jobs usually receive benefits such as paid holidays, vacations, and sick leave and medical insurance.

WORK ENVIRONMENT

Work conditions vary based on the job and employer. Many photographers work a 35- to 40-hour workweek, but freelancers and news photographers often put in long, irregular hours. Commercial and portrait photographers work in comfortable surroundings. Photojournalists seldom are assured physical comfort in their work and may in fact face danger when covering stories on natural disasters or military conflicts. Some photographers work in research laboratory settings; others work on aircraft; and still others work underwater. For some photographers, conditions change from day to day. One day, they may be photographing a hot and dusty rodeo; the next they may be taking pictures of a dog sled race in Alaska.

In general, photographers work under pressure to meet deadlines and satisfy customers. Freelance photographers have the added pressure of uncertain incomes and have to continually seek out new clients.

For specialists in fields such as fashion photography, breaking into the field may take years. Working as another photographer's assistant is physically demanding when carrying equipment is required.

For freelance photographers, the cost of equipment can be quite expensive, with no assurance that the money spent will be repaid through income from future assignments. Freelancers in travel-related photography, such as travel and tourism photographers and photojournalists, have the added cost of transportation and accommodations. For all photographers, flexibility is a major asset.

OUTLOOK

Employment of photographers will increase about as fast as the average for all occupations through 2014, according to the *Occupational Outlook Handbook*. The demand for new images should remain strong in education, communication, entertainment, marketing, and research. As the Internet grows and more newspapers and magazines turn to electronic publishing, demand will increase for photographers to produce digital images. Additionally, as the population grows and many families have more disposable income to spend, the demand should increase for photographers who specialize in portraiture, especially of children.

Photography is a highly competitive field. There are far more photographers than positions available. Only those who are extremely talented and highly skilled can support themselves as self-employed photographers. Many photographers take pictures as a sideline while working another job.

FOR MORE INFORMATION

The ASMP promotes the rights of photographers, educates its members in business practices, and promotes high standards of ethics.
American Society of Media Photographers (ASMP)
150 North Second Street
Philadelphia, PA 19106-1912
Tel: 215-451-2767
http://www.asmp.org

The NPPA maintains a job bank, provides educational information, and makes insurance available to its members. It also publishes News Photographer *magazine.*
National Press Photographers Association (NPPA)
3200 Croasdaile Drive, Suite 306
Durham, NC 27705-2588
Tel: 919-383-7246
Email: info@nppa.org
http://www.nppa.org

This organization provides training, publishes its own magazine, and offers various services for its members.
Professional Photographers of America
229 Peachtree Street, NE, Suite 2200
Atlanta, GA 30303-1608
Tel: 800-786-6277
Email: csc@ppa.com
http://www.ppa.com

For information on student membership, contact
Student Photographic Society
229 Peachtree Street, NE, Suite 2200
Atlanta, GA 30303-1608
Tel: 866-886-5325
Email: info@studentphoto.com
http://www.studentphoto.com

Prepress Workers

OVERVIEW

Prepress workers handle the first stage in the printing process. This initial phase of production involves multiple steps, including creating pages from text and graphics and making printing plates. With the introduction of desktop publishing and other computer technology, the prepress process has changed dramatically over the past decade. Computerized processes have replaced many of the traditional processes, eliminating a number of prepress jobs but opening up new opportunities as well.

According to the U.S. Department of Labor, 141,000 people are employed in prepress jobs. Approximately 42,000 of these jobs are with commercial printing companies. Other jobs are with prepress service bureaus (companies that deal exclusively with prepress work) and newspapers.

HISTORY

The history of modern printing began with the invention of movable type in the 15th century. For several centuries before that, books had been printed from carved wooden blocks or laboriously copied by hand. These painstaking methods of production were so expensive that books were chained to prevent theft.

In the 1440s, Johannes Gutenberg invented a form of metal type that could be used over and over. The first known book to be printed with this movable type was a Bible in 1455—the now-famous Gutenberg Bible. Gutenberg's revolutionary new type greatly

A worker in the prepress department of a printing company makes a plate for an offset printing press. *(Jim West Photography)*

reduced the time and cost involved in printing, and books soon became plentiful.

Ottmar Mergenthaler, a German immigrant to the United States, invented the Linotype machine in 1886. Linotype allowed the typesetter to set type from a keyboard that used a mechanical device to set letters in place. Before this, printers were setting type by hand, one letter at a time, picking up each letter individually from their typecases as they had been doing for more than 400 years. At about the same time, Tolbert Lanston invented the Monotype machine, which also had a keyboard but set the type as individual letters. These inventions allowed compositors to set type much faster and more efficiently.

With these machines, newspapers advanced from the small two-page weeklies of the 1700s to the huge editions of today's metropolitan dailies. The volume of other periodicals, advertisements, books, and other printed matter also proliferated.

In the 1950s, a new system called photocomposition was introduced into commercial typesetting operations. In this system, typesetting machines used photographic images of letters, which were projected onto a photosensitive surface to compose pages. Instructions to the typesetting machine about which letters to project and where to project them were fed in through a punched-paper or magnetic tape, which was, in turn, created by an operator at a keyboard.

Most recently, typesetting has come into the home and office in the form of desktop publishing. This process has revolutionized the industry by enabling companies and individuals to do their own type composition and graphic design work.

THE JOB

Prepress work involves a variety of tasks, most of which are now computer-based. The prepress process is typically broken down into the following areas of responsibility: compositor and typesetter, paste-up worker, desktop publishing specialist, pre-flight technician, output technician, scanner operator, camera operator, lithographic artist, film stripper, and platemaker.

Compositors and *typesetters* are responsible for setting up and arranging type by hand or by computer into galleys for printing. This is done using "cold type" technology (as opposed to the old "hot type" method, which involved using molten lead to create letters and lines of text). A common method is phototypesetting, in which type is entered into a computer and output on photographic film or paper. Typesetting in its traditional sense requires a *paste-up worker* to then position illustrations and lay out columns of type. This manual process is quickly being phased out by desktop publishing.

Most often today, desktop publishing is the first step in the production process. The *desktop publisher* designs and lays out text and graphics on a personal computer according to the specifications of the job. This involves sizing text, setting column widths, and arranging copy with photos and other images. All elements of the piece are displayed on the computer screen and manipulated using a keyboard and mouse. In commercial printing plants, jobs tend to come from customers on computer disk, eliminating the need for initial desktop publishing work on the part of the printing company. (For more information, see the article Desktop Publishing Specialists)

The entire electronic file is reviewed by the *pre-flight technician* to ensure that all of its elements are properly formatted and set up. At small print shops—which account for the majority of the printing industry—a *job printer* is often the person in charge of typesetting, page layout, proofing copy, and fixing problems with files.

Once a file is ready, the *output technician* transmits it through an imagesetter onto paper, film, or directly to a plate. The latter method is called digital imaging, and it bypasses the film stage altogether. Direct-to-plate technology has been adopted by a growing number of printing companies nationwide.

If a file is output onto paper or provided camera-ready, the *camera operator* photographs the material and develops film negatives, either by hand or by machine. Because the bulk of commercial printing today is done using lithography, most camera operators can also be called *lithographic photographers.*

Often it is necessary to make corrections, change or reshape images, or lighten or darken the film negatives. This is the job of the *lithographic artist,* who, depending on the area of specialty, might have the title *dot etcher, retoucher,* or *letterer.* This film retouching work is highly specialized and is all done by hand using chemicals, dyes, and special tools.

The *film stripper* is the person who cuts film negatives to the proper size and arranges them onto large sheets called flats. The pieces are taped into place so that they are in proper position for the plate to be made.

The *platemaker,* also called a *lithographer* because of the process used in most commercial plants, creates the printing plates. This is done using a photographic process. The film is laid on top of a thin metal plate treated with a light-sensitive chemical. It is exposed to ultraviolet light, which "burns" the positive image into the plate. Those areas are then chemically treated so that when ink is applied to the plate, it adheres to the images to be printed and is repelled by the nonprinting areas.

Lithography work traditionally involved sketching designs on stone, clay, or glass. Some of these older methods are still used for specialized purposes, but the predominant method today is the one previously described, which is used in offset printing. In offset printing, a series of cylinders are used to transfer ink from the chemically treated plate onto a rubber cylinder (called a blanket), then onto the paper. The printing plate never touches the paper but is "offset" by the rubber blanket.

If photos and art are not provided electronically, the *scanner operator* scans them using a high-resolution drum or flatbed scanner. In the scanning process, the continuous color tone of the original image is interpreted electronically and converted into a combination of the four primary colors used in printing: cyan (blue), magenta, yellow, and black—commonly called CMYK. A screening process separates the image into the four colors, each of which is represented by a series of dots called a halftone. These halftones are recorded to film from which printing plates are made. During the printing process, ink applied to each of the plates combines on paper to re-create the color of the original image.

REQUIREMENTS

High School

Educational requirements for prepress workers vary according to the area of responsibility, but all require at least a high school diploma, and most call for a strong command of computers.

Whereas prepress areas used to be typesetting and hand-composition operations run by people skilled in particular crafts, they are now predominantly computer-based. Workers are no longer quite as specialized and generally are competent in a variety of tasks. Thus, one of the most important criteria for prepress workers today is a solid base of computer knowledge, ideally in programs and processes related to graphic design and prepress work. Young people interested in the field are advised to take courses in computer science, mathematics, and electronics.

Postsecondary Training

The more traditional jobs, such as camera operator, film stripper, lithographic artist, and platemaker, require longer, more specialized preparation. This might involve an apprenticeship or a two-year associate's degree. But these jobs now are on the decline as they are replaced by computerized processes.

Postsecondary education is strongly encouraged for most prepress positions and a requirement for some jobs, including any managerial role. Graphic arts programs are offered by community and junior colleges as well as four-year colleges and universities. Postsecondary programs in printing technology are also available.

Any programs or courses that give you exposure to the printing field will be an asset. Courses in printing are often available at vocational-technical institutes and through printing trade associations.

Certification or Licensing

The National Council for Skill Standards in Graphic Communications has established a list of competencies for workers in the printing industry. To demonstrate their knowledge, operators can take examinations in flexographic press operation, offset sheetfed and web press operation, finishing and stitching, and imaging. Applicants receive the national council certified operator designation for each examination that they successfully complete.

Other Requirements

Prepress work requires strong communications skills, attention to detail, and the ability to perform well in a high-pressure, deadline-driven environment. Physically, you should have good manual dexterity, good eyesight, and overall visual perception. Artistic skill is an advantage in nearly any prepress job.

EXPLORING

A summer job or internship doing basic word processing or desktop publishing is one way to get a feel for what prepress work involves. Such an opportunity could even be found through a temporary agency. Of course, you will need a knowledge of computers and certain software.

You also can volunteer to do desktop publishing or design work for your school newspaper or yearbook. This would have the added benefit of exposing you to the actual printing process.

EMPLOYERS

There are approximately 141,000 prepress workers employed in the United States. Most prepress work is in firms that do commercial or business printing and in newspaper plants. Other jobs are at companies that specialize in certain aspects of the prepress process, for example, platemaking or outputting of film.

Because printing is so widespread, prepress jobs are available in almost any part of the country. However, according to the *Occupational Outlook Handbook,* prepress work is concentrated in large printing centers like New York, Chicago, Los Angeles-Long Beach, Philadelphia, Minneapolis-St. Paul, Boston, and Washington, D.C.

STARTING OUT

Information on apprenticeships and training opportunities is available through state employment services and local chapters of printing industry associations.

If you wish to start working first and learn your skills on the job you should contact potential employers directly, especially if you want to work in a small nonunion print shop. Openings for trainee positions may be listed in newspaper want ads or with the state employment service. Trade school graduates may find jobs through their school's career services office. And industry association offices often run job listing services.

ADVANCEMENT

Some prepress work, such as typesetting, can be learned fairly quickly; other jobs, like film stripping or platemaking, take years to master. Workers often begin as assistants and move into on-the-job training programs. Entry-level workers are trained by more experienced workers and advance according to how quickly they learn and prove themselves.

In larger companies, prepress workers can move up the ranks to take on supervisory roles. Prepress and production work is also a good starting point for people who aim to become a customer service or sales representative for a printing company.

EARNINGS

Pay rates vary for prepress workers, depending on their level of experience and responsibility, type of company, where they live, and whether or not they are union members. Prepress technicians and workers had median annual earnings of $32,840 in 2005. Salaries ranged from less than $19,430 to $52,800 or more. Mean earnings in commercial printing, the industry employing the largest number of prepress technicians and workers, were $34,820. Those employed in newspaper, book, and directory publishing had mean annual earnings of $33,560.

WORK ENVIRONMENT

Generally, prepress workers work in clean, quiet settings away from the noise and activity of the pressroom. Prepress areas are usually air-conditioned and roomy. Desktop publishers and others who work in front of computer terminals can risk straining their eyes, as well as their backs and necks. Film stripping and other detail-oriented work also can be tiring to the eyes. The chemicals used in platemaking can irritate the skin.

An eight-hour day is typical for most prepress jobs, but frequently workers put in more than eight hours. Prepress jobs at newspapers and financial printers often call for weekend and evening hours.

OUTLOOK

Overall employment in the prepress portion of the printing industry is expected to decline through 2014, according to the U.S. Department of Labor. While it is anticipated that the demand for printed materials will increase, prepress work will not, mainly because of new innovations.

Almost all prepress operations are computerized, and many of the traditional jobs that involved highly skilled handwork—film strippers, paste-up workers, photoengravers, camera operators, and platemakers—are being phased out. The computer-oriented aspects of prepress work have replaced most of these tasks. Employment of desktop publishing specialists, however, is expected to grow faster than the average. Demand for preflight technicians will also be strong. And specialized computer skills will increasingly be needed to handle direct-to-plate and other new technology.

Given the increasing demand for rush print jobs, printing trade service companies should offer good opportunities for prepress workers. Larger companies and companies not equipped for specialized prepress work will continue to turn to these specialty shops to keep up with their workload.

FOR MORE INFORMATION

This organization offers information, services, and training related to printing, electronic prepress, electronic publishing, and other areas of the graphic arts industry.
Graphic Arts Information Network
Printing Industries of America/Graphic Arts Technical Foundation
200 Deer Run Road
Sewickley, PA 15143-2600
Tel: 800-910-4283
Email: gain@piagatf.org
http://www.gain.net

This organization represents U.S. and Canadian workers in all craft and skill areas of the printing and publishing industries. In addition to developing cooperative relationships with employers, it also offers education and training through local union schools.
Graphic Communications Conference of the International Brotherhood of Teamsters
1900 L Street, NW
Washington, DC 20036-5002
Tel: 202-462-1400
http://www.gciu.org

This trade association of graphic communications and graphic arts supplier companies offers economic and management information, publications, and industry reports and studies.
IPA-The Association of Graphic Solutions Providers
7200 France Avenue South, Suite 223
Edina, MN 55435-4309
Tel: 800-255-8141
Email: info@ipa.org
http://www.ipa.org

This graphic arts trade association is a good source of general information.
National Association for Printing Leadership
75 West Century Road
Paramus, NJ 07652-1408
Tel: 800-642-6275
http://www.napl.org

For information on certification, contact
National Council for Skill Standards in Graphic Communications
Harry V. Quadracci Printing & Graphic Center
800 Main Street
Pewaukee, WI 53072-4601
Tel: 262-695-6251
http://www.ncssgc.org

For information on careers and educational institutions, visit
Graphic Comm Central
http://teched.vt.edu/gcc

Printing Press Operators and Assistants

OVERVIEW

Printing press operators and *printing press operator assistants* prepare, operate, and maintain printing presses. Their principal duties include installing and adjusting printing plates, loading and feeding paper, mixing inks and controlling ink flow, and ensuring the quality of the final printed piece.

There are approximately 191,000 printing press operators in the United States. They are mostly employed by newspaper plants and commercial and business printers.

HISTORY

The forerunners of today's modern printing presses were developed in Germany in the 15th century. They made use of the new concept of movable type, an invention generally credited to Johannes Gutenberg. Before Gutenberg's time, most books were copied by hand or printed from carved wooden blocks. Movable type used separate pieces of metal that could be easily set in place, locked into a form for printing, and then used again for another job.

The first presses consisted of two flat surfaces. Once set in place, the type was inked with a roller, and a sheet of paper was pressed against the type with a lever. Two people working together could print about 300 pages a day.

In the early 19th century, Friedrich Konig, another German, developed the first cylinder press. With a cylinder press, the paper is mounted on a large cylinder that is rolled over a flat printing surface.

The first rotary press was developed in the United States in 1865 by William Bullock. On this kind of press, the inked surface is on a revolving cylinder called a plate cylinder. The plate cylinder acts like a roller and prints onto a continuous sheet of paper (called a web) coming off a giant roll.

The speed and economy of the web press was improved by the discovery of offset printing in the early 20th century. In this process, the raised metal type used in earlier processes was substituted with a flexible plate that could be easily attached to the plate cylinder. The ink is transferred from the plate onto a rubber cylinder (called a blanket), then onto the paper. The printing plate never touches the paper but is "offset" by the rubber blanket.

Offset printing uses the process of lithography, in which the plate is chemically treated so that ink sticks only to the parts that are to be printed and is repelled by the nonprint areas.

Offset lithography is the most common form of printing today and is used on both web-fed and sheet-fed presses. Web-fed presses are used for newspapers and other large-volume, lower-cost runs. The fastest web presses today can print about 150,000 complete newspapers in an hour. Sheet-fed presses, which print on single sheets of paper rather than a continuous roll, are used for smaller, higher-quality jobs.

Other forms of printing are gravure (in which depressions on an etched plate are inked and pressed to paper), flexography (a form of rotary printing using flexible rubber plates with raised image areas and fast-drying inks), and letterpress (the most traditional method, in which a plate with raised, inked images is pressed against paper).

THE JOB

The duties of press operators and their assistants vary according to the size of the printing plant in which they work. Generally, they are involved in all aspects of making the presses ready for a job and monitoring and operating the presses during the print run. Because most presses now are computerized, the work of press operators involves both electronic and manual processes.

In small shops, press operators usually handle all of the tasks associated with running a press, including cleaning and oiling the parts and making minor repairs. In larger shops, press operators are aided by assistants who handle most maintenance and cleanup tasks.

Once the press has been inspected and the printing plate arrives from the platemaker, the "makeready" process begins. In this stage, the operators mount the plates into place on the printing surface or cylinder. They mix and match the ink, fill the ink fountains, and adjust the ink flow and dampening systems. They also load the paper, adjust the press to the paper size, feed the paper through the cylinders and, on a web press, adjust the tension controls. When this is done, a proof sheet is run off for the customer's review.

When the proof has been approved and final adjustments have been made, the press run begins. During the run, press operators constantly check the quality of the printed sheets and make any necessary adjustments. They look to see that the print is clear and properly positioned and that ink is not offsetting (blotting) onto other sheets. If the job involves color, they make sure that the colors line up properly with the images they are assigned to (registration). Operators also monitor the chemical properties of the ink and correct temperatures in the drying chamber, if the press has one.

On a web press, the feeding and tension mechanisms must be continually monitored. If the paper tears or jams, it must be rethreaded. As a roll of paper runs out, a new one must be spliced onto the old one. Some web presses today can print up to 50,000 feet an hour. At this rate, the press might run through a giant roll of paper every half hour. In large web printing plants, it takes an entire crew of specialized operators to oversee the process.

Most printing plants now have computerized printing presses equipped with sophisticated instrumentation. Press operators work at a control panel that monitors the printing processes and can adjust each variable automatically.

REQUIREMENTS

High School

The minimum educational requirement for printing press operators and assistants is a high school diploma. Students interested in this field should take courses that offer an introduction to printing and color theory, as well as chemistry, computer science, electronics, mathematics, and physics—any course that develops mechanical and mathematical aptitude.

Postsecondary Training

Traditionally, press operators learned their craft through apprenticeship programs ranging from four to five years. Apprenticeships are still available, but they are being phased out by postsecondary programs in printing equipment operation offered by technical and trade schools and community and junior colleges. Information on apprenticeships is often available through state employment services and local chapters of printing industry associations. Additionally, many press operators and assistants still receive informal on-the-job training after they are hired by a printer.

Computer training is also essential to be successful in the printing industry today. With today's rapid advances in technology, "students need all the computer knowledge they can get," advises John Smotherman, press operator and shift supervisor at Busch and Schmidt Company in Broadview, Illinois.

Certification or Licensing

The National Council for Skill Standards in Graphic Communications has established a list of competencies—what an operator should know and be able to do—for the expert level of performance. Skill standards are available for electronic imaging, sheetfed and web offset press, flexographic press, and finishing and stitching. Operators who take one or more examination in these subjects areas can receive the designation national council certified operator.

Other Requirements

Strong communication skills, both verbal and written, are a must for press operators and assistants. They also must be able to work well as a team, both with each other and with others in the printing company. Any miscommunication during the printing process can be costly if it means re-running a job or any part of it. Working well under pressure is another requirement because most print jobs run on tight deadlines.

EXPLORING

High school is a good time to begin exploring the occupation of printing press operator. Some schools offer print shop classes, which provide the most direct exposure to this work. Working on the high school newspaper or yearbook is another way to gain a familiarity with the printing process. A delivery job with a print shop or a visit to a local printing plant will offer you the chance to see presses in action and get a feel for the environment in which press operators work. You also might consider a part-time, temporary, or summer job as a cleanup worker or press feeder in a printing plant.

EMPLOYERS

There are approximately 191,000 press operators employed in the United States. The bulk of these are with newspapers and commercial and business printers. Companies range from small print shops, where one or two press operators handle everything, to large corporations that employ teams of press operators to work around the clock.

Other press operator jobs are with in-plant operations, that is, in companies and organizations that do their own printing in-house.

Because printing is so geographically diverse, press operator jobs are available in almost any city or town in the country. However, according to the *Occupational Outlook Handbook,* press work is concentrated in large printing centers like New York, Chicago, Los Angeles-Long Beach, Philadelphia, Minneapolis-St. Paul, Boston, and Washington, D.C.

STARTING OUT

Openings for trainee positions may be listed in newspaper want ads or with the state employment service. Trade school graduates may find jobs through their school's career services office. And industry association offices often run job listing services.

John Smotherman notes that many young people entering the field start out in a part-time position while still in school. "I think students should pursue all the classroom education they can, but many intricacies of the printing process, like how certain inks and papers work together, need to be learned through experience," he says.

ADVANCEMENT

Most printing press operators, even those with some training, begin their careers doing entry-level work, such as loading, unloading, and cleaning the presses. In large print shops, the line of promotion is usually as follows: press helper, press assistant, press operator, press operator-in-charge, press room supervisor, superintendent.

Press operators can advance in salary and responsibility level by learning to work more complex printing equipment, for example by moving from a one-color press to a four-color press. Printing press operators should be prepared to continue their training and education throughout their careers. As printing companies upgrade their equipment and buy new, more computerized presses, retraining will be essential.

Employment By Industry

Field	Employment	Mean Annual Earnings
Printing and related support activities	102,090	$33,550
Newspaper, book, and directory publishers	19,510	$36,280
Converted paper product manufacturing	14,990	$34,220
Advertising and related services	6,460	$27,560
Federal government	870	$65,120

Source: U.S. Department of Labor, 2005

Press operators who are interested in other aspects of the printing business also may find advancement opportunities elsewhere in their company. Those with business savvy may be successful in establishing their own print shops.

EARNINGS

Pay rates vary for press operators, depending on their level of experience and responsibility, type of company, where they live, and whether or not they are union members. Median annual earnings of press operators were $30,730 in 2005, according to the U.S. Department of Labor (USDL). Salaries ranged from less than $18,450 to $49,870 or more. The USDL reports the following annual mean earnings for printing press operators by industry: printing and related support activities, $35,550; newspaper, book, and directory publishing, $36,280; converted paper product manufacturing, $34,220; and advertising and related services, $27,560.

WORK ENVIRONMENT

Pressrooms are well ventilated, well lit, and humidity controlled. They are also noisy. Often press operators must wear ear protectors. Press work can be physically strenuous and requires a lot of standing. Press operators also have considerable contact with ink and cleaning fluids that can cause skin and eye irritation.

Working around large machines can be hazardous, so press operators must constantly observe good safety habits.

An eight-hour day is typical for most press operators, but some work longer hours. Smaller plants generally have only a day shift, but many larger plants and newspaper printers run around the clock. At these plants, like in hospitals and factories, press operator shifts are broken into day, afternoon/evening, and "graveyard" hours.

OUTLOOK

The U.S. Department of Labor predicts that employment of press operators will grow more slowly than the average for all occupations through 2014. An increased demand for printed materials—advertising, direct mail pieces, computer software packaging, books, and magazines—will be offset by the use of larger, more efficient machines. Additionally, new business practices such as printing-on-demand (where materials are printed in smaller amounts as they are requested by customers instead of being printed in large runs that may not be used) and electronic publishing (which is the publication of materials on the Internet or through other electronic methods of dissemination) will also limit opportunities for workers in this field.

Newcomers to the field are likely to encounter stiff competition from experienced workers or workers who have completed retraining programs to update their skills. Opportunities are expected to be greatest for students who have completed formal apprenticeships or postsecondary training programs.

FOR MORE INFORMATION

For information on flexographic printing, contact
Flexographic Technical Association
900 Marconi Avenue
Ronkonkoma, NY 11779-7212
Tel: 631-737-6020
http://www.flexography.org

This organization offers information, services, and training related to printing, electronic prepress, electronic publishing, and other areas of the graphic arts industry.
Graphic Arts Information Network
Printing Industries of America/Graphic Arts Technical Foundation
200 Deer Run Road
Sewickley, PA 15143-2600
Tel: 800-910-4283

Email: gain@piagatf.org
http://www.gain.net

This organization represents U.S. and Canadian workers in all craft and skill areas of the printing and publishing industries. In addition to developing cooperative relationships with employers, it also offers education and training through local union schools.

Graphic Communications Conference of the International Brotherhood of Teamsters
1900 L Street, NW
Washington, DC 20036-5002
Tel: 202-462-1400
http://www.gciu.org

This trade association of graphic communications and graphic arts supplier companies offers economic and management information, publications, and industry reports and studies.

IPA-The Association of Graphic Solutions Providers
7200 France Avenue South, Suite 223
Edina, MN 55435-4309
Tel: 800-255-8141
Email: info@ipa.org
http://www.ipa.org

This graphic arts trade association is a good source of general information.

National Association for Printing Leadership
75 West Century Road
Paramus, NJ 07652-1408
Tel: 800-642-6275
http://www.napl.org

For more information on the national council certified operator designation, contact

National Council for Skill Standards in Graphic Communications
Harry V. Quadracci Printing & Graphic Center
800 Main Street
Pewaukee WI 53072-4601
Tel: 262-695-6251
http://www.ncssgc.org

For information on careers and educational institutions, visit

Graphic Comm Central
http://teched.vt.edu/gcc

Printing Sales Representatives

OVERVIEW

A *printing sales representative* is a printing company's front-line operator, the person in charge of visiting companies and other prospective clients to solicit their print business. A salesperson in printing may represent a commercial printer, a business printer, a magazine and book printer, or a company that specializes in one aspect of the industry, such as binding. The job of sales representative can be stressful but highly rewarding, both professionally and financially. There are approximately 21,000 printing sales representatives employed in the United States.

HISTORY

The history of the printing industry dates back centuries and is filled with revolutionary innovations, each improving the speed and efficiency of the printing process. Less is known about the origin and development of the job of printing sales representative.

Of course, as long as commercial printing has been in existence, there have been print sales. The concept of employees dedicated full time to selling print, however, is fairly modern. Traditionally, most owners of printing companies did the selling themselves, relates Bob Saluga, a longtime sales representative at Service Web Corporation in Chicago, Illinois. This is still true at some small print shops, although many small shops use brokers or simply market themselves and let the customers come to them.

There was also a time, Saluga adds, when the plant manager often acted as salesperson. When a prospective customer requested

A printing sales representative prepares an estimate for a customer. (Jim West Photography)

a presentation, the plant manager would quickly put on a tie and sport coat and make the call.

Today most printing sales representatives are devoted entirely to selling, although many also manage a multiple-member sales team.

THE JOB

Printing sales representatives are the lifeblood of the companies they represent. They are responsible for identifying prospective customers and securing their printing business. As with nearly any sales job, this process is ongoing, both in the search for new clients and in maintaining relationships with clients they already have.

There are several ways salespeople find customers. One is researching companies they think are a good fit with the specific printing services they offer and making "cold calls." Another is following up on referrals they get from existing clients or other sources. As in any business, networking is crucial.

Once they have leads, printing reps then make sales calls. These calls might be general, letting the prospective customer know what services their printing company can offer, or they might be in response to a specific job a customer needs printed. If a specific job is being discussed, the sales rep helps the client determine the job's parameters and then provides an estimate of how much it will cost to be printed. Most companies request bids from two or three different print vendors.

Once a job is procured, the role of the sales representative is by no means over. Printing salespeople are assisted by *customer service representatives,* who oversee much of the production work, but the salesperson continues to be the main conduit between the customer and the company. They must communicate with both parties every step of the way to make sure that the customer is satisfied with the quality of the job. This means establishing good relationships with not only the customers, but with the staff in the printing plant who do the hands-on work.

"The sales force is the engine that drives the car," says Jim Hortsman, a sales representative for Moss Printing Company in Chicago, Illinois. "But we depend on the parts to make it work."

REQUIREMENTS
High School
In printing, a person with only a high school diploma is likely to get a job as a sales representative only if they have a history of work in the printing industry. High school courses that will be helpful to you in your work as a printing sales representative include business, speech, mathematics, and computer science.

Postsecondary Training
Most often, a college degree is the minimum educational requirement for printing sales representatives. Four-year college programs in graphic arts and/or marketing and finance are recommended.

Other Requirements
Printing sales representatives must have strong written and verbal communication skills and the ability to interact well with people.

"It is important for sales representatives to be team players," says Jim Reinhardt, a sales representative for Wicklander Printing Corporation in Chicago, Illinois. "There are lots of people involved in the process, so you have to be flexible and communicative."

Successful salespeople are also persuasive, have an outgoing and enthusiastic personality, are highly energetic and motivated, and perform well under pressure.

EXPLORING
If you are interested in becoming a printing sales representative, try to get part-time or summer work in a retail store. Working as

a telemarketer also is useful. Some high schools and junior colleges offer programs that combine classroom study with work experience in sales.

EMPLOYERS

Approximately 21,000 printing sales representatives are employed in the United States. Printing sales jobs may be with commercial or business printers, magazine or book printers, trade shops, or binderies.

Because printing is so widespread, sales jobs are available in most parts of the country. However, according to the *Occupational Outlook Handbook*, printing work is concentrated in large printing centers like New York, Chicago, Los Angeles-Long Beach, Philadelphia, Minneapolis-St. Paul, Boston, and Washington, D.C.

STARTING OUT

Traditionally, most printing sales reps started in entry-level production jobs and rose through the ranks to sales. This is still a common way to move into the job of sales representative. Often, working as a customer service representative or prepress specialist can be a stepping-stone to a sales job.

Today it is possible to get a job as printing sales representative directly out of school, with a business-related degree like marketing, for example, or a degree in graphic arts. But printing is a highly technical industry, and a salesperson must have a solid understanding of printing processes and technology to be successful. That is why many companies choose to promote staff from within rather than train a new person.

Young people looking for jobs in print sales should check newspaper want ads and job placement listings through local chapters of printing associations.

ADVANCEMENT

Often printing sales representatives will start out with a few of a company's smaller accounts and take on more as they prove their success.

"As a sales representative, you have a lot of control over your income," Jim Reinhardt says. "Generally speaking, the harder you work, the more you sell."

Sales representatives at printing companies with a large sales force also have the opportunity to advance to the position of *sales manager.* In that capacity, they oversee the work of the entire sales team, establishing goals, setting quotas and territories, arranging for training the sales force in new technology and techniques, and analyzing marketing and sales statistics to improve policies and practices.

EARNINGS

The salary of printing sales representatives can vary greatly, depending on how they are compensated and how successful they are. Some sales reps are paid straight commission, and others might be paid a mix of salary and bonuses. Newcomers and trainees might expect to be placed on straight salary until they are up and running.

According to the *Career Guide to Industries,* printing sales representatives had median hourly earnings of $25.20 (or $52,416 annually) in 2004. Printing sales reps typically earn between $30,000 and $75,000 annually, but the most successful salespeople can make more than $100,000 a year.

WORK ENVIRONMENT

Most industry sources say that printing sales reps spend about 70 percent of their time out of the office, traveling locally, regionally, or nationally to visit clients and make sales calls. A sales rep might report to the office in the morning, check in on the jobs he or she is currently overseeing, handle any problems or other matters that need attending to, make calls or write letters, and then head out for the bulk of the day. No day is the same as the next, which means there really is no typical work environment or structure.

Hours vary as well, although most veteran print salespeople put in well over 40 hours a week. On average, printing sales reps work about 50 hours, but some log as many as 80 hours in a week.

"This is not a career for people who are never willing to put in more than 40 hours a week," Jim Reinhardt says.

OUTLOOK

According to the U.S. Department of Labor, employment of sales representatives, as a group, is expected to grow as fast as the average for all occupations through 2014, in response to growth of the services industries employing them.

Despite recent predictions of a "paperless society," the demand for printed products is increasing rather than decreasing. This means that there will be a growing need for printing sales representatives in the near future.

Because of the competitive nature of the printing industry, the role of the salesperson is critical to a company's success and offers much opportunity. "If you value quality and are willing to put in the extra work, you can be successful," Jim Reinhardt says.

FOR MORE INFORMATION

This organization offers information, services, and training related to printing, electronic prepress, electronic publishing, and other areas of the graphic arts industry.
Graphic Arts Information Network
Printing Industries of America/Graphic Arts Technical Foundation
200 Deer Run Road
Sewickley, PA 15143-2600
Tel: 800-910-4283
Email: gain@piagatf.org
http://www.gain.net

This trade association of graphic communications and graphic arts supplier companies offers economic and management information, publications, and industry reports and studies.
IPA-The Association of Graphic Solutions Providers
7200 France Avenue South, Suite 223
Edina, MN 55435-4309
Tel: 800-255-8141
Email: info@ipa.org
http://www.ipa.org

This graphic arts trade association is a good source of general information.
National Association for Printing Leadership
75 West Century Road
Paramus, NJ 07652-1408
Tel: 800-642-6275
http://www.napl.org

For information on careers and educational institutions, visit
Graphic Comm Central
http://teched.vt.edu/gcc

INTERVIEW

Louis Segovia is a sales executive/account executive for United Graphics, Inc., a commercial printing company in Chicago, Illinois. He has worked in the field for 18 years. Louis discussed his career with the editors of Careers in Focus: Publishing.

Q. Why did you decide to enter this career?

A. I entered the printing industry because the opportunity presented itself as a entry-level position. I decided to get into sales because of the unlimited earnings potential.

Q. What advice would you give to high school students who are interested in this career?

A. Students should take graphic arts and graphic design courses. Those interested in sales should take sales and marketing classes and work on their public speaking skills. They should also work for the school newspaper or at a print shop to gain hands-on experience.

Q. What are the three most important professional qualities for people in your career?

A. Good organization skills, good communication skills, and persistence.

Q. What do you like most and least about your job?

A. I enjoy meeting new people, traveling, and the varying daily routine. Least appealing is the occasional rejection from customers, dealing with unrealistic demands from customers, and the pressure of meeting sales goals.

Reporters

OVERVIEW

Reporters are the foot soldiers for newspapers, magazines, and television and radio broadcast companies. They gather and analyze information about current events and write stories for publication or for broadcasting. News analysts, reporters, and correspondents hold approximately 64,000 jobs in the United States.

HISTORY

Newspapers are the primary disseminators of news in the United States. People read newspapers to learn about the current events that are shaping their society and societies around the world. Newspapers give public expression to opinion and criticism of government and societal issues, and, of course, provide the public with entertaining, informative reading.

Newspapers are able to fulfill these functions because of the freedom given to the press. However, this was not always the case. The first American newspaper, published in 1690, was suppressed four days after it was published. And it was not until 1704 that the first continuous newspaper appeared.

One early newspaperman who later became a famous writer was Benjamin Franklin. Franklin worked for his brother at a Boston newspaper before publishing his own paper two years later in 1723 in Philadelphia.

A number of developments in the printing industry made it possible for newspapers to be printed more cheaply. In the late 19th century, new types of presses were developed to increase production, and more importantly, the Linotype machine was invented. The Linotype mechanically set letters so that handset type was no longer necessary.

QUICK FACTS

School Subjects
English
Journalism

Personal Skills
Communication/ideas
Helping/teaching

Work Environment
Indoors and outdoors
Primarily multiple locations

Minimum Education Level
Bachelor's degree

Salary Range
$18,300 to $32,270 to $71,220+

Certification or Licensing
None available

Outlook
More slowly than the average

DOT
131

GOE
11.08.02

NOC
5123

O*NET-SOC
27-3022.00

Reporters interview an executive from the Ford Motor Company at the North American International Auto Show. *(Jim West Photography)*

This dramatically decreased the amount of prepress time needed to get a page into print. Newspapers could respond to breaking stories more quickly, and late editions with breaking stories became part of the news world.

These technological advances, along with an increasing population, factored into the rapid growth of the newspaper industry in the United States. In 1776, there were only 37 newspapers in the United States. Today there are more than 1,460 daily and nearly 6,700 weekly newspapers in the country.

As newspapers grew in size and widened the scope of their coverage, it became necessary to increase the number of employees and to assign them specialized jobs. Reporters have always been the heart of newspaper staffs. However, in today's complex world, with the public hungry for news as it occurs, reporters and correspondents are involved in all media—not only newspapers, but magazines, radio, and television as well. Today, with the advent of the Internet, many newspapers have gone online, causing many reporters to become active participants on the Information Superhighway.

THE JOB

Reporters collect information on newsworthy events and prepare stories for newspaper or magazine publication or for radio or television broadcast. The stories may simply provide information about local, state, or national events, or they may present opposing points of view on issues of current interest. In this latter capacity, the press plays an important role in monitoring the actions of public officials and others in positions of power.

Stories may originate as an assignment from an editor or as the result of a lead, or news tip. Good reporters are always on the lookout for good story ideas. To cover a story, they gather and verify facts by interviewing people involved in or related to the event, examining documents and public records, observing events as they happen, and researching relevant background information. Reporters generally take notes or use a tape recorder as they collect information and write their stories once they return to their offices. In order to meet a deadline, they may have to telephone the stories to *rewriters,* who write or transcribe the stories for them. After the facts have been gathered and verified, the reporters transcribe their notes, organize their material, and determine what emphasis, or angle, to give the news. The story is then written to meet prescribed standards of editorial style and format.

The basic functions of reporters are to observe events objectively and impartially, record them accurately, and explain what the news means in a larger, societal context. Within this framework, there are several types of reporters.

The most basic is the *news reporter.* This job sometimes involves covering a beat, which means that the reporter may be assigned to consistently cover news from an area such as the local courthouse, police station, or school system. It may involve receiving general assignments, such as a story about an unusual occurrence or an obituary of a community leader. Large daily papers may assign teams of reporters to investigate social, economic, or political events and conditions.

Many newspaper, wire service, and magazine reporters specialize in one type of story, either because they have a particular interest in the subject or because they have acquired the expertise to analyze and interpret news in that particular area. *Topical reporters* cover stories for a specific department, such as medicine, politics, foreign affairs, sports, consumer affairs, finance, science, business, education, labor, or religion. They sometimes write features explaining the history that has led up to certain events in the field they cover. *Feature writers* generally write longer, broader stories than news reporters, usually on more upbeat subjects, such as fashion, art, theater, travel, and social events. They may write about trends, for example, or profile local celebrities. *Editorial writers* and *syndicated news columnists* present viewpoints that, although based on a thorough knowledge, are opinions on topics of popular interest. *Columnists* write under a byline and usually specialize in a particular subject, such as politics or government activities. *Critics* review restaurants, books, works of art, movies, plays, musical performances, and other cultural events.

Specializing allows reporters to focus their efforts, talent, and knowledge on one area of expertise. It also gives them more opportunities to develop deeper relationships with contacts and sources, which is necessary to gain access to the news.

Correspondents report events in locations distant from their home offices. They may report news by mail, telephone, fax, or computer from rural areas, large cities throughout the United States, or countries. Many large newspapers, magazines, and broadcast companies have one correspondent who is responsible for covering all the news for the foreign city or country where they are based. These reporters are known as *foreign correspondents*.

Reporters on small or weekly newspapers not only cover all aspects of the news in their communities, but also may take photographs, write editorials and headlines, lay out pages, edit wire-service copy, and help with general office work.

REQUIREMENTS

High School

High school courses that will provide you with a firm foundation for a reporting career include English, journalism, history, social studies, communications, typing, and computer science. Speech courses will help you hone your interviewing skills, which are necessary for success as a reporter. In addition, it will be helpful to take college prep courses, such as foreign language, math, and science.

Postsecondary Training

You will need at least a bachelor's degree to become a reporter, and a graduate degree will give you a great advantage over those entering the field with lesser degrees. Most editors prefer applicants with degrees in journalism because their studies include liberal arts courses as well as professional training in journalism. Some editors consider it sufficient for a reporter to have a good general education from a liberal arts college. Others prefer applicants with an undergraduate degree in liberal arts and a master's degree in journalism. The great majority of journalism graduates hired today by newspapers, wire services, and magazines have majored specifically in news-editorial journalism.

More than 400 colleges offer programs in journalism leading to a bachelor's degree. In these schools, around three-fourths of a student's time is devoted to a liberal arts education and one-fourth to the professional study of journalism, with required courses such as introductory mass media, basic reporting and copyediting, history of journalism, and press law and ethics. Students are encouraged to select other journalism courses according to their specific interests.

Journalism courses and programs are also offered by many community and junior colleges. Graduates of these programs are prepared to go to work directly as general assignment reporters, but they may encounter difficulty when competing with graduates of four-year programs. Credit earned in community and junior colleges may be transferable to four-year programs in journalism at other colleges and universities. Journalism training may also be obtained in the armed forces. Names and addresses of newspapers and a list of journalism schools and departments are published in the annual *Editor & Publisher International Year Book: The Encyclopedia of the Newspaper Industry* (New York: Editor & Publisher) which is available for reference in most public libraries and newspaper offices.

A master's degree in journalism may be earned at approximately 120 schools, and a doctorate at about 35 schools. Graduate degrees may prepare students specifically for careers in news or as journalism teachers, researchers, and theorists, or for jobs in advertising or public relations.

A reporter's liberal arts training should include courses in English (with an emphasis on writing), sociology, political science, economics, history, psychology, business, speech, and computer science. Knowledge of foreign languages is also useful. To be a reporter in a specialized field, such as science or finance, requires concentrated course work in that area.

Other Requirements

In order to succeed as a reporter, it is crucial that you have typing skill, as you will type your stories using word processing programs. Although not essential, a knowledge of shorthand or speedwriting makes note taking easier, and an acquaintance with news photography is an asset.

You must also be inquisitive, aggressive, persistent, and detail-oriented. You should enjoy interaction with people of various races, cultures, religions, economic levels, and social statuses.

EXPLORING

You can explore a career as a reporter in a number of ways. You can talk to reporters and editors at local newspapers and radio and TV stations. You can interview the admissions counselor at the school of journalism closest to your home.

In addition to taking courses in English, journalism, social studies, speech, computer science, and typing, high school students can acquire practical experience by working on school newspapers or on a church, synagogue, or mosque newsletter. Part-time and summer jobs on newspapers provide invaluable experience to the aspiring reporter.

College students can develop their reporting skills in the laboratory courses or workshops that are part of the journalism curriculum. College students might also accept jobs as campus correspondents for selected newspapers. People who work as part-time reporters covering news in a particular area of a community are known as *stringers* and are paid only for those stories that are printed.

More than 3,000 journalism scholarships, fellowships, and assistantships are offered by universities, newspapers, foundations, and professional organizations to college students. Many newspapers and magazines offer summer internships to journalism students to provide them with practical experience in a variety of basic reporting and editing duties. Students who successfully complete internships are usually placed in jobs more quickly upon graduation than those without such experience.

EMPLOYERS

Of the approximately 64,000 reporters and correspondents employed in the United States, approximately 61 percent work for newspaper, periodical, book, and directory publishers. About 25 percent work in radio and television broadcasting. The rest are employed by wire services.

STARTING OUT

Jobs in this field may be obtained through college career services offices or by applying directly to the personnel departments of individual employers. If you have some practical experience, you will have an advantage; you should be prepared to present a portfolio of material you wrote as a volunteer or part-time reporter, or other writing samples.

Most journalism school graduates start out as general assignment reporters or copy editors for small publications. A few outstanding journalism graduates may be hired by large city newspapers or national magazines. They are trained on the job. But they are the exception, as large employers usually require several years' experience. As a rule, novice reporters cover routine assignments, such as reporting on civic and club meetings, writing obituaries, or summarizing speeches. As you become more skilled in reporting, you will be assigned to more important events or to a regular beat, or you may specialize in a particular field.

ADVANCEMENT

Reporters may advance by moving to larger newspapers or press services, but competition for such positions is unusually keen. Many highly qualified reporters apply for these jobs every year.

A select number of reporters eventually become columnists, correspondents, editorial writers, editors, or top executives. These important and influential positions represent the top of the field, and competition is strong for them.

Many reporters transfer the contacts and knowledge developed in newspaper reporting to related fields, such as public relations, advertising, or preparing copy for radio and television news programs.

EARNINGS

There are great variations in the earnings of reporters. Salaries are related to experience, the type of employer for which the reporter works, geographic location, and whether the reporter is covered by a contract negotiated by the Newspaper Guild.

According to the U.S. Department of Labor, the median salary for reporters and correspondents was $32,270 in 2005. The lowest paid 10 percent of these workers earned $18,300 or less per year, while the highest paid 10 percent made $71,220 or more annually. Mean annual earnings for reporters employed in newspaper, book, and directory publishing were $36,770 in 2005; reporters employed in Internet publishing had mean annual earnings of $41,940.

According to the Newspaper Guild, the average top minimum salary for reporters under a Guild contract was $48,380 in 2006. Salaries ranged from $21,790 to $ 84,580 or more.

WORK ENVIRONMENT

Reporters work under a great deal of pressure in settings that differ from the typical business office. Their jobs generally require a five-day, 35- to 40-hour week, but overtime and irregular schedules are

Employment By Industry

Field	Employment	Mean Annual Earnings
Newspaper, book, and directory publishers	39,520	$36,770
Radio and television broadcasting	9,290	$49,990
Other information services	1,800	$55,410
Internet publishing and broadcasting	220	$41,940

Source: U.S. Department of Labor, 2005

very common. Reporters employed by morning papers start work in the late afternoon and finish around midnight, while those on afternoon or evening papers start early in the morning and work until early or mid-afternoon. Foreign correspondents often work late at night to send the news to their papers in time to meet printing deadlines.

The day of the smoky, ink-stained newsroom has passed, but newspaper offices are still hectic places. Reporters have to work amid the clatter of computer keyboards and other machines, loud voices engaged in telephone conversations, and the bustle created by people hurrying about. An atmosphere of excitement prevails, especially as press deadlines approach.

Travel is often required in this occupation, and some assignments may be dangerous, such as covering wars, political uprisings, fires, floods, and other events of a volatile nature.

OUTLOOK

Employment for reporters and correspondents is expected to grow more slowly than the average for all occupations through 2014, according to the *Occupational Outlook Handbook*. While the number of self-employed reporters and correspondents is expected to grow, newspaper jobs are expected to decrease because of mergers, consolidations, and closures in the newspaper industry.

Because of an increase in the number of small community and suburban daily and weekly newspapers, opportunities will be best for journalism graduates who are willing to relocate and accept relatively low starting salaries. With experience, reporters on these small papers can move up to editing positions or may choose to transfer to reporting jobs on larger newspapers or magazines.

Openings will be limited on big city dailies. While individual papers may enlarge their reporting staffs, little or no change is expected in the total number of these newspapers. Applicants will face strong competition for jobs on large metropolitan newspapers. Experience is a definite requirement, which rules out most new graduates unless they possess credentials in an area for which the publication has a pressing need. Occasionally, a beginner can use contacts and experience gained through internship programs and summer jobs to obtain a reporting job immediately after graduation.

A significant number of jobs will be provided by magazines, but the major news magazines generally prefer experienced reporters. Stronger employment growth is expected for reporters in online newspapers and magazines.

Overall, the prospects are best for graduates who have majored in news-editorial journalism and completed an internship while in school. The top graduates in an accredited program will have a great advantage, as will talented technical and scientific writers. Small newspapers prefer to hire beginning reporters who are acquainted with the community and are willing to help with photography and other aspects of production. Without at least a bachelor's degree in journalism, applicants will find it increasingly difficult to obtain even an entry-level position.

Those with doctorates and practical reporting experience may find teaching positions at four-year colleges and universities, while highly qualified reporters with master's degrees may obtain employment in journalism departments of community and junior colleges.

Poor economic conditions do not drastically affect the employment of reporters and correspondents. Their numbers are not severely cut back even during a downturn; instead, employers forced to reduce expenditures will suspend new hiring.

FOR MORE INFORMATION

For a list of accredited programs in journalism and mass communications, visit the ACEJMC Web site
Accrediting Council on Education in Journalism and Mass Communications (ACEJMC)
University of Kansas School of Journalism and Mass Communications
Stauffer-Flint Hall, 1435 Jayhawk Boulevard
Lawrence, KS 66045-7575

Tel: 785-864-3973
http://www.ku.edu/~acejmc/STUDENT/PROGLIST.SHTML

This organization provides general educational information on all areas of journalism.
Association for Education in Journalism and Mass Communication
234 Outlet Pointe Boulevard
Columbia, SC 29210-5667
Tel: 803-798-0271
Email: aejmchq@aejmc.org
http://www.aejmc.org

To read The Journalist's Road to Success: A Career Guide, *which lists schools offering degrees in news-editing, and financial aid to those interested in print journalism, visit the DJNF Web site*
Dow Jones Newspaper Fund (DJNF)
PO Box 300
Princeton, NJ 08543-0300
Tel: 609-452-2820
Email: newsfund@wsj.dowjones.com
http://djnewspaperfund.dowjones.com

For information on careers in newspapers and industry facts and figures, contact
Newspaper Association of America
1921 Gallows Road, Suite 600
Vienna, VA 22182-3900
Tel: 703-902-1600
Email: IRC@naa.org
http://www.naa.org

For information on union membership, contact
Newspaper Guild-Communication Workers of America
501 Third Street, NW, Suite 250
Washington, DC 20001-2797
Tel: 202-434-7177
Email: guild@cwa-union.org
http://www.newsguild.org

Contact the society for information on student chapters, scholarships, educational information, discussion groups, and much more.
Society of Professional Journalists
Eugene S. Pulliam National Journalism Center
3909 North Meridian Street

Indianapolis, IN 46208-4011
Tel: 317-927-8000
http://spj.org

Visit the following Web site for comprehensive information on journalism careers, summer programs, and college journalism programs.
High School Journalism
http://www.highschooljournalism.org

For comprehensive information for citizens, students, and news people about the field of journalism, visit:
Project for Excellence in Journalism
http://www.journalism.org

Webmasters

OVERVIEW

Webmasters design, implement, and maintain Web sites for newspapers, magazines, and other publishers; corporations; educational institutions; not-for-profit organizations; government agencies; or other institutions. Webmasters should have working knowledge of network configurations, interface, graphic design, software development, business, writing, marketing, and project management. Because the function of a webmaster encompasses so many different responsibilities, the position is often held by a team of individuals in a large organization.

HISTORY

The Internet developed from ARPANET, an experimental computer network established in the 1960s by the U.S. Department of Defense. By the late 1980s, the Internet was being used by many government and educational institutions.

The World Wide Web was the brainchild of physicist Tim Berners-Lee. Although Berners-Lee formed his idea of the Web in 1989, it was another four years before the first Web browser (Mosaic) made it possible for people to navigate the Web simply. Businesses quickly realized the commercial potential of the Web and soon developed their own Web sites.

No one person or organization is in charge of the Internet and what's on it. However, each Web site needs an individual, or team of workers, to gather, organize, and maintain online data. These specialists, called webmasters, manage sites for businesses of all sizes (including publishing companies), nonprofit organizations, schools, government agencies, and private individuals.

QUICK FACTS

School Subjects
Computer science
Mathematics

Personal Skills
Communication/ideas
Technical/scientific

Work Environment
Primarily indoors
Primarily one location

Minimum Education Level
Some postsecondary training

Salary Range
$38,030 to $65,000 to
 $108,561

Certification or Licensing
Voluntary

Outlook
Much faster than the average

DOT
030

GOE
11.01.01

NOC
2175

O*NET-SOC
N/A

THE JOB

Because the idea of designing and maintaining a Web site is relatively new, there is no complete, definitive job description for webmasters. Many of their job responsibilities depend on the goals and needs of the particular organization for which they work. There are, however, some basic duties that are common to almost all webmasters.

Webmasters, specifically site managers, first secure space on the Web for the site they are developing. This is done by contracting with an Internet service provider. The provider serves as a sort of storage facility for the organization's online information, usually charging a set monthly fee for a specified amount of megabyte space. The webmaster may also be responsible for establishing a uniform resource locator, or URL, for the Web site he or she is developing. The URL serves as the site's online "address" and must be registered with InterNIC, the Web URL registration service.

The webmaster is responsible for developing the actual Web site for his or her organization. In some cases, this may involve actually writing the text content of the pages. More commonly, however, the webmaster is given the text to be used and is merely responsible for programming it in such a way that it can be displayed on a Web page. In larger companies webmasters specialize in content, adaptation, and presentation of data.

In order for text to be displayed on a Web page, it must be formatted using hypertext markup language (HTML). HTML is a system of coding text so that the computer that is "reading" it knows how to display it. For example, text could be coded to be a certain size or color or to be italicized or boldface. Paragraphs, line breaks, alignment, and margins are other examples of text attributes that must be coded in HTML.

Although it is less and less common, some webmasters code text manually, by actually typing the various commands into the body of the text. This method is time consuming, however, and mistakes are easily made. More often, webmasters use a software program that automatically codes text. Some word processing programs, such as WordPerfect, even offer HTML options.

Along with coding the text, the webmaster must lay out the elements of the Web site in such a way that it is visually pleasing, well organized, and easy to navigate. He or she may use various colors, background patterns, images, tables, or charts. These graphic elements can come from image files already on the Web, software clip art files, or images scanned into the computer with an electronic scanner. In some cases, when an organization is using the Web site to promote its product or service, the webmaster may work with a marketing specialist or department to develop a page.

Some Web sites have several directories or "layers." That is, an organization may have several Web pages, organized in a sort of "tree," with its home page connected, via hypertext links, to other pages, which may in turn be linked to other pages. The webmaster is responsible for organizing the pages in such a way that a visitor can easily browse through them and find what he or she is looking for. Such webmasters are called *programmers* and *developers;* they are also responsible for creating Web tools and special Web functionality.

For webmasters who work for organizations, such as a major publisher, that have several different Web sites, one responsibility may be making sure that the "style" or appearance of all the pages is the same. This is often referred to as "house style." In large organizations, such as universities, where many different departments may be developing and maintaining their own pages, it is especially important that the webmaster monitor these pages to ensure consistency and conformity to the organization's requirements. In almost every case, the webmaster has the final authority for the content and appearance of his or her organization's Web site. He or she must carefully edit, proofread, and check the appearance of every page.

Besides designing and setting up Web sites, most webmasters are charged with maintaining and updating existing sites. Most sites contain information that changes regularly. Some change daily or even hourly. Depending on his or her employer and the type of Web site, the webmaster may spend a good deal of time updating and remodeling the page. He or she is also responsible for ensuring that the hyperlinks contained within the Web site lead to the sites they should. Since it is common for links to change or become obsolete, the webmaster usually performs a link check every few weeks.

Other job duties vary, depending on the employer and the position. Most webmasters are responsible for receiving and answering email messages from visitors to the organization's Web site. Some webmasters keep logs and create reports on when and how often their pages are visited and by whom. Depending on the company, Web sites count anywhere from 300 to 1.4 billion visits, or "hits," a month. Some create and maintain order forms or online "shopping carts" that allow visitors to the Web site to purchase products or services. Some may train other employees on how to create or update Web pages. Finally, webmasters may be responsible for developing and adhering to a budget for their departments.

REQUIREMENTS

High School

High school students who are interested in becoming webmasters should take as many computer science classes as they can. Mathematics classes are also helpful. Finally, because writing skills are important in this career, English classes are good choices.

Postsecondary Training

A number of community colleges, colleges, and universities offer classes and certificate programs for webmasters, but there is no standard educational path or requirement for becoming a webmaster. While many have bachelor's degrees in computer science, information systems, or computer programming, liberal arts degrees, such as English, are not uncommon. There are also webmasters who have degrees in engineering, mathematics, and marketing.

Certification or Licensing

There is strong debate within the industry regarding certification. Some, mostly corporate chief executive officers, favor certification. They view certification as a way to gauge an employee's skill and Web mastery expertise. Others argue, however, that it is nearly impossible to test knowledge of technology that is constantly changing and improving. Despite the split of opinion, webmaster certification programs are available at many colleges, universities, and technical schools throughout the United States. Programs vary in length, anywhere from three weeks to nine months or more. Topics covered include client/server technology, Web development, programs, and software and hardware. The International Webmasters Association and World Organization of Webmasters also offer voluntary certification programs.

Should webmasters be certified? Though it's currently not a prerequisite for employment, certification can only enhance a candidate's chance at landing a webmaster position.

What most webmasters have in common is a strong knowledge of computer technology. Most people who enter this field are already well versed in computer operating systems, programming languages, computer graphics, and Internet standards. When considering candidates for the position of webmaster, employers usually require at least two years of experience with Internet technologies. In some cases, employers require that candidates already have experience in designing and maintaining Web sites. It is, in fact, most common for someone to move into the position of webmaster from another computer-related job in the same organization.

Other Requirements

Webmasters should be creative. It is important for a Web page to be well designed in order to attract attention. Good writing skills and an aptitude for marketing are also excellent qualities for anyone considering a career in Web site design.

Although much of the webmaster's day may be spent alone, it is nonetheless important that he or she be able to communicate and work well with others. Depending on the organization for which he or she works, the Webmaster may have periodic meetings with graphic designers, marketing specialists, online producers, writers, or other professionals who have input into the Web site development. In many larger organizations, there is a team of webmasters rather than just one. Although each team member works alone on his or her own specific duties, the members may meet frequently to discuss and coordinate their activities.

EXPLORING

One of the easiest ways to learn about what a webmaster does is to spend time surfing the World Wide Web. By examining a variety of Web sites to see how they look and operate, you can begin to get a feel for what goes into a home page.

An even better way to explore this career is to design your own personal Web page. Many Internet servers offer their users the option of designing and maintaining a personal Web page for a very low fee. A personal page can contain virtually anything that you want to include, from snapshots of friends to audio files of favorite music to hypertext links to other favorite sites.

EMPLOYERS

The majority of webmasters working today are full-time employees, according to *Interactive Week*. They are employed by publishing companies, Web design companies, businesses, schools or universities, not-for-profit organizations, government agencies—in short, any organization that requires a presence on the World Wide Web. Webmasters may also work as freelancers or operate their own Web design businesses.

STARTING OUT

Most people become webmasters by moving into the position from another computer-related position within the same company. Since most large organizations already use computers for various functions, they may employ a person or several people to serve as computer "specialists." If these organizations decide to develop their own Web sites, they frequently assign the task to one of these employees who is already experienced with the computer system. Often, the person who ultimately becomes an organization's webmaster at first just takes on the job in addition to his or her other, already established duties.

Another way that individuals find jobs in this field is through online postings of job openings. Many companies post webmaster position openings online because the candidates they hope to attract are very likely to use the Internet for a job search. Therefore, the prospective webmaster should use the World Wide Web to check job-related newsgroups. He or she might also use a Web search engine to locate openings.

ADVANCEMENT

Experienced webmasters employed by a large organization may be able to advance to the position of *online producer*. These workers supervise a team of webmasters and are responsible for every aspect of a company's presence on the Web. Others might advance by starting their own business, designing Web sites on a contract basis for several clients rather than working exclusively for one organization.

Opportunities for webmasters of the future are endless due to the continuing development of online technology. As understanding and use of the World Wide Web increase, there may be new or expanded job duties in the future for individuals with expertise in this field.

EARNINGS

According to Salary.com, salaries for webmasters in 2006 ranged from $30,030 to $108,561. However, many webmasters move into the position from another position within their company or have taken on the task in addition to other duties. These employees are often paid approximately the same salary they were already making.

According to the National Association of Colleges and Employers, the starting salary for graduates with a bachelor's degree in computer science was $50,820 in 2005; in management information systems, $44,417; and in information sciences and systems, $44,775.

Depending on the organization for which they work, webmasters may receive a benefits package in addition to salary. A typical benefits package would include paid vacations and holidays, medical insurance, and perhaps a pension plan.

WORK ENVIRONMENT

Although much of the webmaster's day may be spent alone, it is nonetheless important that he or she be able to communicate and work well with others. Depending on the organization for which he or she works, the webmaster may have periodic meetings with graphic designers, marketing specialists, online producers, editors, writers, or other professionals who have input into Web site development. In many larger organizations, there is a team of webmasters rather than just one. Although each team member works alone on his or her own specific duties, the members may meet frequently to discuss and coordinate their activities.

Because technology changes so rapidly, this job is constantly evolving. Webmasters must spend time reading and learning about new developments in online communication. They may be continually working with new computer software or hardware. Their actual job responsibilities may even change, as the capabilities of both the organization and the World Wide Web itself expand. It is important that these employees be flexible and willing to learn and grow with the technology that drives their work.

Because they don't deal with the general public, most webmasters are allowed to wear fairly casual attire and to work in a relaxed atmosphere. In most cases, the job calls for standard working hours, although there may be times when overtime is required.

OUTLOOK

According to the U.S. Department of Labor, the field of computer and data processing services is projected to be among the fastest growing industries for the next decade. As a result, the employment rate of webmasters and other computer specialists is expected to grow much faster than the average rate for all occupations through 2014. As more and more businesses, not-for-profit organizations, educational institutions, and government agencies choose to "go online," the total number of Web sites will grow, as will the need for experts to design them. Many companies view Web sites as important and necessary business and marketing tools.

One thing to keep in mind, however, is that when technology advances extremely rapidly, it tends to make old methods of doing things obsolete. If current trends continue, the responsibilities of the webmaster will be carried out by a group or department instead of a single employee, in order to keep up with the demands of the position. It is possible that in the next few years, changes in technology will make the Web sites we are now familiar with a thing of the past.

Another possibility is that, like desktop publishing, user-friendly software programs will make Web site design so easy and efficient that it no longer requires an "expert" to do it well. Webmasters who are concerned with job security should be willing to continue learning and using the very latest developments in technology, so that they are prepared to move into the future of online communication, whatever it may be.

FOR MORE INFORMATION

For information on training and certification programs, contact the following organizations

International Webmasters Association
119 East Union Street, Suite F
Pasadena, CA 91103-3952
Tel: 626-449-3709
http://www.iwanet.org

World Organization of Webmasters
9580 Oak Avenue Parkway, Suite 7-177
Folsom, CA 95630-1888
Tel: 916-989-2933
Email: info@joinwow.org
http://www.joinwow.org

Writers

OVERVIEW

Writers express, edit, promote, and interpret ideas and facts in written form for books, magazines, trade journals, newspapers, technical studies and reports, company newsletters, radio and television broadcasts, and advertisements.

Writers develop fiction and nonfiction ideas for plays, novels, poems, and other related works; report, analyze, and interpret facts, events, and personalities; review art, music, film, drama, and other artistic presentations; and persuade the general public to choose or favor certain goods, services, and personalities. There are approximately 192,000 salaried writers, authors, and technical writers employed in the United States.

HISTORY

The skill of writing has existed for thousands of years. Papyrus fragments with writing by ancient Egyptians date from about 3000 B.C., and archaeological findings show that the Chinese had developed books by about 1300 B.C. A number of technical obstacles had to be overcome before printing and the profession of writing evolved. Books of the Middle Ages were copied by hand on parchment. The ornate style that marked these books helped ensure their rarity. Also, few people were able to read. Religious fervor prohibited the reproduction of secular literature.

The development of the printing press by Johannes Gutenberg in the middle of the 15th century and the liberalism of the Protestant Reformation, which encouraged a wide range of publications, greater literacy, and the creation of a number of works of literary

QUICK FACTS

School Subjects
English
Journalism

Personal Skills
Communication/ideas
Helping/teaching

Work Environment
Primarily indoors
Primarily one location

Minimum Education Level
Bachelor's degree

Salary Range
$24,320 to $46,420 to $89,940+

Certification or Licensing
None available

Outlook
About as fast as the average

DOT
131

GOE
01.01.02

NOC
5121

O*NET-SOC
27-3042.00, 27-3043.01, 27-3043.02, 27-3043.03, 27-3043.04

Horror writer Stephen King signs a copy of his latest book at a bookstore in London. *(Rune Hellestad/UPI/Landov)*

merit, prompted the development of the publishing industry. The first authors worked directly with printers.

The modern publishing age began in the 18th century. Printing became mechanized, and the novel, magazine, and newspaper developed. The first newspaper in the American colonies appeared in the early 18th century, but it was Benjamin Franklin who, as editor and writer, made the *Pennsylvania Gazette* one of the most influential in setting a high standard for his fellow American journalists. Franklin also published the first magazine in the colonies, *The American Magazine,* in 1741.

Advances in the printing trades, photoengraving, retailing, and the availability of capital produced a boom in newspapers and magazines in the 19th century. Further mechanization in the printing field, such as the use of the Linotype machine, high-speed rotary presses, and special color reproduction processes, set the stage for still further growth in the book, newspaper, and magazine industry.

In addition to the print media, the broadcasting industry has contributed to the development of the professional writer. Film, radio, and television are sources of entertainment, information, and education that provide employment for thousands of writers.

THE JOB

Writers work in the field of communications. Specifically, they deal with the written word, whether it is destined for the printed page, broadcast, computer screen, or live theater. The nature of their work is as varied as the materials they produce: books, magazines, trade journals, newspapers, technical reports, company newsletters and other publications, advertisements, speeches, scripts for motion picture and stage productions, and scripts for radio and television broadcast. Writers develop ideas and write for all media.

Prose writers for newspapers, magazines, and books share many of the same duties. First they come up with an idea for an article or book from their own interests or are assigned a topic by an editor. The topic is of relevance to the particular publication. (For example, a writer for a magazine on parenting may be assigned an article on car seat safety.) Then writers begin gathering as much information as possible about the subject through library research, interviews, the Internet, observation, and other methods. They keep extensive notes from which they draw material for their project. Once the material has been organized and arranged in logical sequence, writers prepare a written outline. The process of developing a piece of writing is exciting, although it can also involve detailed and solitary work. After researching an idea, a writer might discover that a different perspective or related topic would be more effective, entertaining, or marketable.

When working on assignment, writers submit their outlines to an editor or other company representative for approval. Then they write a first draft of the manuscript, trying to put the material into words that will have the desired effect on their audience. They often rewrite or polish sections of the material as they proceed, always searching for just the right way of imparting information or expressing an idea or opinion. A manuscript may be reviewed, corrected, and revised numerous times before a final copy is submitted. Even after that, an editor may request additional changes.

Writers for newspapers, magazines, or books often specialize in their subject matter. Some writers might have an educational background that allows them to give critical interpretations or analyses. For example, a health or science writer for a newspaper typically has a degree in biology and can interpret new ideas in the field for the average reader.

Columnists or *commentators* analyze news and social issues. They write about events from the standpoint of their own experience or opinion. *Critics* review literary, musical, or artistic works and performances. *Editorial writers* write on topics of public interest, and their comments, consistent with the viewpoints and policies of their employers, are intended to stimulate or mold public opinion. *Newswriters* work for newspapers, radio, or TV news departments, writing news stories from notes supplied by reporters or wire services.

Corporate writers and writers for nonprofit organizations have a wide variety of responsibilities. These writers may work in such places as a large media company or for a small nonprofit religious group, where they may be required to write news releases, annual reports, speeches for the company president, or public relations materials. Typically they are assigned a topic with length requirements for a given project. They may receive raw research materials, such as statistics, and they are expected to conduct additional research, including personal interviews. These writers must be able to write quickly and accurately on short deadlines, while also working with people whose primary job is not in the communications field. The written work is submitted to a supervisor and often a legal department for approval; rewrites are a normal part of this job.

Copywriters write copy that is primarily designed to sell goods and services. Their work appears as advertisements in newspapers, magazines, and other publications or as commercials on radio and television broadcasts. Sales and marketing representatives first provide information on the product and help determine the style and length of the copy. The copywriters conduct additional research and interviews; to formulate an effective approach, they study advertising trends and review surveys of consumer preferences. Armed with this information, copywriters write a draft that is submitted to the account executive and the client for approval. The copy is often returned for correction and revision until everyone involved is satisfied. Copywriters, like corporate writers, may also write articles, bulletins, news releases, sales letters, speeches, and other related informative and promotional material. Many copywriters are employed in advertising agencies. They also may work for public relations firms or in communications departments of large companies.

Technical writers can be divided into two main groups: those who convert technical information into material for the general public, and those who convey technical information between professionals. Technical writers in the first group may prepare service manuals or handbooks, instruction or repair booklets, or sales literature or brochures; those in the second group may write grant proposals, research reports, contract specifications, or research abstracts.

Playwrights do similar writing for the stage. They write dialogue and describe action for plays that may be tragedies, comedies, or dramas, with themes sometimes adapted from fictional, historical, or narrative sources. Playwrights combine the elements of action, conflict, purpose, and resolution to depict events from real or imaginary life. They often make revisions even while the play is in rehearsal.

Novelists and *short story writers* create stories that may be published in books, magazines, or literary journals. They take incidents from their own lives, from news events, or from their imaginations and create characters, settings, actions, and resolutions. *Poets* create narrative, dramatic, or lyric poetry for books, magazines, or other publications, as well as for special events such as commemorations. These writers may work with literary agents or editors who help guide them through the writing process, which includes research of the subject matter and an understanding of the intended audience. Many universities and colleges offer graduate degrees in creative writing. In these programs, students work intensively with published writers to learn the art of storytelling.

Writers can be employed either as in-house staff or as freelancers. Pay varies according to experience and the position, but freelancers must provide their own office space and equipment such as computers and fax machines. Freelancers also are responsible for keeping tax records, sending out invoices, negotiating contracts, and providing their own health insurance.

REQUIREMENTS

High School

While in high school, build a broad educational foundation by taking courses in English, literature, foreign languages, history, general science, social studies, computer science, and typing. The ability to type is almost a requisite for all positions in the communications field, as is familiarity with computers.

Postsecondary Training

Competition for writing jobs almost always demands the background of a college education. Many employers prefer you have a broad liberal arts background or majors in English, literature, history, philosophy, or one of the social sciences. Other employers desire communications or journalism training in college. Occasionally a master's degree in a specialized writing field may be required. A number of schools offer courses in journalism, and some of them offer courses or majors in book publishing, publication management, and newspaper and magazine writing.

In addition to formal course work, most employers look for practical writing experience. If you have served on high school or college newspapers, yearbooks, or literary magazines, or if you have worked for small community newspapers or radio stations, even in an unpaid position, you will be an attractive candidate. Many book publishers, magazines, newspapers, and radio and television stations have summer internship programs that provide valuable training if you want to learn about the publishing and broadcasting businesses. Interns do many simple tasks, such as running errands and answering phones, but some may be asked to perform research, conduct interviews, or even write some minor pieces.

Writers who specialize in technical fields may need degrees, concentrated course work, or experience in specific subject areas. This applies frequently to engineering, business, or one of the sciences. Also, technical communications is a degree now offered at many universities and colleges.

If you wish to enter positions with the federal government, you will have to take a civil service examination and meet certain specified requirements, according to the type and level of position.

Other Requirements

To be a writer, you should be creative and able to express ideas clearly, have a broad general knowledge, be skilled in research techniques, and be computer literate. Other assets include curiosity, persistence, initiative, resourcefulness, and an accurate memory. For some jobs—on a newspaper, for example, where the activity is hectic and deadlines are short—the ability to concentrate and produce under pressure is essential.

EXPLORING

As a high school or college student, you can test your interest and aptitude in the field of writing by serving as a reporter or writer on school newspapers, yearbooks, and literary magazines. Various writing courses and workshops will provide the opportunity to sharpen your writing skills.

Small community newspapers and local radio stations often welcome contributions from outside sources, although they may not have the resources to pay for them. Jobs in bookstores, magazine shops, and even newsstands will offer you a chance to become familiar with various publications.

You can also obtain information on writing as a career by visiting local newspapers and publishers and interviewing some of the writers who work there. Career conferences and other guidance programs frequently include speakers on the entire field of communications from local or national organizations.

EMPLOYERS

There are approximately 142,000 writers and authors and 50,000 technical writers currently employed in the United States. Approximately half of salaried writers and editors work in the information sector, which includes newspapers, magazines, book publishers, radio and television broadcasting, software publishers, and Internet businesses. Writers also work for advertising agencies and public relations firms and work on journals and newsletters published by business and nonprofit organizations, such as professional associations, labor unions, and religious organizations. Other employers are government agencies and film production companies.

STARTING OUT

A fair amount of experience is required to gain a high-level position in the field. Most writers start out in entry-level positions. These jobs may be listed with college career services offices, or they may be obtained by applying directly to the employment departments of the individual publishers or broadcasting companies. Graduates who previously served internships with these companies often have the advantage of knowing someone who can give them a personal recommendation. Want ads in newspapers and trade journals are another source for jobs. Because of the competition for positions, however, few vacancies are listed with public or private employment agencies.

Employers in the communications field usually are interested in samples of published writing. These are often assembled in an organized portfolio or scrapbook. Bylined or signed articles are more credible (and, as a result, more useful) than stories whose source is not identified.

Entry-level positions as a junior writer usually involve library research, preparation of rough drafts for part or all of a report, cataloging, and other related writing tasks. These are generally carried on under the supervision of a senior writer.

Some technical writers have entered the field after working in public relations departments or as technicians or research assistants, then transferring to technical writing as openings occur. Many firms now hire writers directly upon application or recommendation of college professors and career services offices.

ADVANCEMENT

Most writers find their first jobs as editorial or production assistants. Advancement may be more rapid in small companies, where beginners learn by doing a little bit of everything and may be given writing tasks immediately. In large firms, duties are usually more compartmentalized. Assistants in entry-level positions are assigned such tasks as research, fact checking, and copyrighting, but it generally takes much longer to advance to full-scale writing duties.

Promotion into more responsible positions may come with the assignment of more important articles and stories to write, or it may be the result of moving to another company. Mobility among employees in this field is common. An assistant in one publishing house may switch to an executive position in another. Or a writer may switch to a related field as a type of advancement.

A technical writer can be promoted to positions of responsibility by moving from such jobs as writer to technical editor to project leader or documentation manager. Opportunities in specialized positions also are possible.

Freelance or self-employed writers earn advancement in the form of larger fees as they gain exposure and establish their reputations.

EARNINGS

In 2005, median annual earnings for salaried writers and authors were $46,420 a year, according to the U.S. Department of Labor. The lowest 10 percent earned less than $24,320, while the highest 10 percent earned $89,940 or more. In book publishing, some specialties pay better than others. Technical writers earned a median salary of $55,160 in 2005, with entry-level salaries averaging around $41,000 a year.

In addition to their salaries, many writers earn some income from freelance work. Part-time freelancers may earn from $5,000 to $15,000 a year. Freelance earnings vary widely. Full-time established freelance writers may earn more than $75,000 a year.

Books to Read

Bly, Robert W. *Careers for Writers & Others Who Have a Way with Words.* 2d ed. New York: McGraw-Hill, 2003.

Connolly, William G., and Allan M. Siegal. *The New York Times Manual of Style and Usage: The Official Style Guide Used by the Writers and Editors of the World's Most Authoritative Newspaper.* New York: Three Rivers Press, 2002.

Gibaldi, Joseph. *MLA Style Manual and Guide to Scholarly Publishing.* 2d ed. New York: Modern Language Association of America, 1998.

Gross, Gerald. *Editors on Editing: What Writers Need to Know About What Editors Do.* 3d rev. ed. New York: Grove Press, 1994.

Microsoft Corporation. *The Microsoft Manual of Style for Technical Publications.* 3d ed. Redmond, Wash.: Microsoft Press, 2003.

Rude, Carolyn D. *Technical Editing.* 4th ed. Reading, Mass.: Longman, 2005.

Shertzer, Margaret. *The Elements of Grammar.* Reading, Mass.: Longman, 1996.

Strunk, William Jr., and E. B. White. *The Elements of Style.* 4th ed. Boston: Allyn & Bacon, 1999.

Trottier, David. *The Freelance Writer's Bible: Your Guide to a Profitable Writing Career Within One Year.* Los Angeles, Calif.: Silman-James Press, 2006.

University of Chicago. *The Chicago Manual of Style: The Essential Guide for Writers, Editors, and Publishers.* 15th ed. Chicago, Ill.: The University of Chicago Press, 2003.

WORK ENVIRONMENT

Working conditions vary for writers. Although their workweek usually runs 35 to 40 hours, many writers work overtime. A publication that is issued frequently has more deadlines closer together, creating greater pressures to meet them. The work is especially hectic on newspapers and at broadcasting companies, which operate seven days a week. Writers often work nights and weekends to meet deadlines or to cover a late-developing story.

Most writers work independently, but they often must cooperate with artists, photographers, rewriters, and advertising people who may have widely differing ideas of how the materials should be prepared and presented.

Physical surroundings range from comfortable private offices to noisy, crowded newsrooms filled with other workers typing and talking on the telephone. Some writers must confine their research to the library or telephone interviews, but others may travel to other cities or countries or to local sites, such as theaters, ballparks, airports, factories, or other offices.

The work is arduous, but most writers are seldom bored. Some jobs, such as that of the foreign correspondent, require travel. The most difficult element is the continual pressure of deadlines. People who are the most content as writers enjoy and work well with deadline pressure.

OUTLOOK

The employment of writers is expected to increase at an average rate through 2014, according to the U.S. Department of Labor. Competition for writing jobs has been and will continue to be competitive. The demand for writers by newspapers, periodicals, book publishers, and nonprofit organizations is expected to increase. The growth of online publishing on company Web sites and other online services will also create a demand for many talented writers; those with computer skills will be at an advantage as a result. Advertising and public relations will also provide job opportunities.

The major book and magazine publishers, broadcasting companies, advertising agencies, public relations firms, and the federal government account for the concentration of writers in large cities such as New York, Chicago, Los Angeles, Boston, Philadelphia, San Francisco, and Washington, D.C. Opportunities with small newspapers, corporations, and professional, religious, business, technical, and trade publications can be found throughout the country.

People entering this field should realize that the competition for jobs is extremely keen. Beginners may have difficulty finding employment. Of the thousands who graduate each year with degrees in English, journalism, communications, and the liberal arts, intending to establish a career as a writer, many turn to other occupations when they find that applicants far outnumber the job openings available. College students would do well to keep this in mind and prepare for an unrelated alternate career in the event they are unable to obtain a position as writer; another benefit of this approach is that, at the same time, they will become qualified as writers in a specialized field. The practicality of preparing for alternate careers is borne out by the fact that opportunities are best in firms that prepare business and trade publications and in technical writing. Job candidates with good writing skills and knowledge of a specialized area such as economics, finance, computer programming, or science will have the best chances of finding jobs.

Potential writers who end up working in a different field may be able to earn some income as freelancers, selling articles, stories, books, and possibly TV and movie scripts, but it is usually difficult for writers to support themselves entirely on independent writing.

FOR MORE INFORMATION

For information on careers in newspaper reporting, education, and financial aid opportunities, contact
American Society of Journalists and Authors
1501 Broadway, Suite 302
New York, NY 10036-5505
Tel: 212-997-0947
http://www.asja.org

For information on science writing and editing, contact
National Association of Science Writers
PO Box 890
Hedgesville, WV 25427-0890
Tel: 304-754-5077
http://www.nasw.org

This organization offers student memberships for those interested in opinion writing.
National Conference of Editorial Writers
3899 North Front Street
Harrisburg, PA 17110-1583
Tel: 717-703-3015
Email: ncew@pa-news.org
http://www.ncew.org

For information on scholarships and student memberships aimed at those preparing for a career in technical communication, contact
Society for Technical Communication
901 North Stuart Street, Suite 904
Arlington, VA 22203-1822
Tel: 703-522-4114
Email: stc@stc.org
http://www.stc.org

INTERVIEW

Laura Agee is a writer in Wichita, Kansas. She currently writes about Christian music for various online and print publications. Laura discussed her career with the editors of Careers in Focus: Publishing.

Q. Why did you decide to become a writer?

A. Though I may have entered journalism at first because I was good at writing, I have found it is now what I love. I have to be honest and say I never dreamed journalism would ever become a full-time career. The concept of writing something and getting paid for it was the furthest thing from my mind when I was a senior in high school. I actually wanted to be a veterinarian.

As a high school senior, I shadowed a local veterinarian and thought I would make money caring for animals. It was my heart's passion at that time. My only problem was that I hated math and I wasn't particularly good at science, and both are needed in veterinary medicine. Seeing that veterinary medicine wasn't in my future, my parents wisely asked me to consider what other passions I loved and perhaps pursue those. I sat down and did some serious thinking and realized that I loved to write, even if I had not written any articles before—save a class assignment or two.

I decided to attend a junior college close to where I lived and took some journalism classes. It was toward the end of my first year of college that the journalism professor saw I had potential. He liked some of the things I wrote in class and asked me to consider being on the school's magazine staff.

Possibilities of working in journalism really came into focus for me as a result of me joining the magazine staff. I built on that experience, and it later led to offers of being asked to be features editor at the four-year Baptist college I transferred to; internships with the Kansas-Nebraska Convention of Southern Baptists and the Billy Graham Evangelistic Association; landing an interview with veteran Christian artist, Margaret Becker; and talking to many other Christian artists such as Nichole Nordeman and Mike Weaver, of Big Daddy Weave.

Q. How/where did you get your first job in this field?

A. My very first job in journalism actually literally fell into my lap, which most of the time, doesn't happen. I was still in college, a senior graduating, when I won third place for Excellence in Features Writing from the Oklahoma Collegiate Press Association. The managing editor at the *Independence Daily Reporter* called me about a week or two after I received that award and wanted me to work for the newspaper.

It was right around the same time that I was accepted for an internship at the Billy Graham Evangelistic Association (BGEA) in Minneapolis for a month, so I turned down the managing editor at the paper. My internship ended a month later. The managing editor of the newspaper called me a week after I finished the BGEA internship and offered me a job as a reporter on staff, and I accepted. But, I never really considered it a "first" job. I have been writing about Christian musicians for awhile and interning for several different places before I took the reporting job, so it was natural and didn't feel awkward at all. It was my first time writing professionally for someone in a job that actually paid—writing articles that weren't about Christian music.

As far as freelancing strictly about Christian music, I got my start by asking. I knew a DJ at K-Love [a contemporary Christian radio station] whom I had worked with at the Billy Graham Evangelistic Association, and I simply asked him if he knew of anyone who would take freelance articles about Christian musicians. He gave me Mark Weber's name. Mark has been a guest numerous times on "The 700 Club" and had written more than 500 articles on Christian music for *CrossWalk, CCM,* and other publications. Mark had heard about my work at the Billy Graham Evangelistic Association and wanted me to write articles for his Web site. He particularly liked one of my first articles I wrote for him, interviewing Tom Pellerin, lead singer for the band, Overflow, that he sent the article to a friend. That friend, I later discovered, was the music guide at the Christian music site at About.com. I was asked to write for Christian music at about.com and have been writing for its music guide, Kim Jones, ever since.

Q. What are the pros/cons of being a music writer?

A. I'll start with the cons first because I like to end on a positive note. Writing can be very exhausting sometimes mentally, thinking about just the right word to use in an article. And, journalism is not for those who want to "make the big bucks." Journalists don't make lots of money. The hours are long, and you work when you are sick, tired, and generally don't feel like writing and because you are a professional with deadlines to meet. Generally, since I more or less write for myself freelancing, I set my own deadlines. Those deadlines aren't as strict as the ones I had for newspaper articles, but still, I have deadlines to meet. Working as a music writer for yourself is actually harder because you have to push yourself, motivate yourself, and get your articles written without anyone telling you, "you need to get this written!"

Sometimes, it is tough doing a phone interview because plenty can go wrong. A recorder can lose power in the middle of an interview, there is poor phone reception when a musician is talking on their cell phone or, sometimes, no matter how I try, I simply cannot understand a word here or there on a digital recording from a phone interview. It is harder to capture emotion from a phone interview or interview done through e-mail because you cannot see the artist's facial expressions when they tell you something. All these factors come into play to sometimes make interviews a challenge to record and also transcribe later on.

Now, the pros. Writing about Christian music is actually fun for me because I decide who I interview. I can pick and choose and if I have trouble scheduling an interview with a Christian musician because of traveling, performing conflicts, etc., I can choose not to interview at that time, pick someone else, and later get back with them for an interview. I have received free CDs, T-shirts, etc. for writing about Christian music and have gotten into concerts and other events for free. When I actually talk to the Christian artists on the phone or via e-mail, I learn so much more from them than I would just attending one of their concerts. I am able to capture their personality better and write a better article as a result. Plus, my work as a Christian music writer has allowed me to forge friendships with some Christian artists that go beyond a one-time, 30-minute interview.

Q. What advice would you give high school students who are interested in this career?

A. If you are truly interested in journalism, shadow a journalist. They can teach you the basics about journalism and how to be flexible as a writer, which is needed whether you write about Christian music or the local dog show that is in town for the weekend. Shadowing can also give you a good idea (after talking with a journalist) if journalism is something you still want to pursue as a full-time career.

Don't be afraid to ask questions. The only stupid question is the one you didn't ask. It is part of learning. And don't be afraid to ask a question in an interview that you don't have written down anywhere. Many times, I won't write down a single question I ask a Christian artist as I am interviewing because I find that I sometimes have a tendency to ask the same questions over and over to different artists. I try to tailor my questions to the artist, coming up with questions the artist hasn't answered. But if you are just starting to write, I would suggest writing down questions so you don't get nervous and forget what you wanted to ask. Musicians sometimes don't have long to talk to you. As you get more experienced interviewing (I have written more than 500 articles), you can forego writing down the questions, if you wish.

Be careful of making your writing too specialized. When I worked at the newspaper, there was a high school girl who wanted to go into journalism. After talking to her, I found what she really wanted was to write poetry. Wanting to write poetry is great, but make sure there is a market for what you want to write. Make sure there is someone who will publish what you are writing, otherwise, you have a nice hobby instead of a career. And don't be afraid to write something even if it initially isn't what you have an interest in. As a features editor, I wrote many articles. Many had nothing to do with Christian music. It taught me how to be flexible and versatile and helped me develop many loves I didn't realize I had. It also taught me basic skills of how to interview people, and those skills were helpful when I came across people who were just extremely shy.

Don't be discouraged if someone will publish what you write, but won't pay you for it. Many publications do not pay for freelance work, but some do. You just have to ask the individual publication. You want to know if you may write stories for a Christian music publication or any publication: Ask, ask, ask around. Many times, networking with people is a great way to open doors to opportunities. It is a great tool for making contacts and learning at the same time. It can also be a great way to develop friendships.

Don't forget to do a little research before you interview someone. It helps to know a little bit about the person you will be talking to in order to know what questions to ask in an interview. It also makes you look more professional by showing the artist that you are interested in their work because you completed research about them on the Internet and through books and magazines, etc.

Don't let your fear of rejection or failure stand in the way of asking someone for something. Some of the best lessons I learned (and am still learning) are because I failed either in my pursuit of something or failed to do something. Failure is what molds and shapes what is still unwritten, and it is how we gain character and learn humility. Just because you may fail once, twice, or more times, doesn't mean you are automatically a failure. It just means you are still learning.

Index

Page numbers in **bold** indicate major treatment of a topic.